DESIGN WITH FLOWERS...*Unlimited*

DESIGN
WITH FLOWERS
...Unlimited

Patricia Kroh

All Flower Arrangements by the Author

Doubleday & Company, Inc., Garden City, New York

To my mother
KATHERINE NADELL KROH
in loving memory

Acknowledgments

I am deeply grateful to the many people and organizations who have been directly or indirectly responsible for helping me make this book possible.

Photographs by Adrien Boutrelle, Stephan Fay, Frederick Cassebeer, Robert H. Ford, William Kaschel and my husband, Milton B. Freudenheim

Line drawings by Edward DiNunzio

Special flowers by Larchmont Nurseries and "Flowers by Lilyan"

Ikebana International Society of New York and Tokyo
Federated Garden Clubs of New York State, Inc.
National Council of State Garden Clubs, Inc.
Horticultural Society of New York, Inc.
Margaret Lord Barnie
Mrs. Henry Kincaid
Mrs. Noel Gaubert—California Garden Clubs, Inc.
Barbara Hodges, Honolulu, Hawaii
Mr. Reikichi Yokohama, Tokyo, Japan
Mr. Mitsuo Tanaka, Consulate General of Japan
Dr. Koto Matsudaira, Ambassador, Permanent Mission of Japan to the United Nations

Contents

Color Illustrations

Black and White Illustrations

DESIGN WITH FLOWERS... *Unlimited*

Introduction

The title of this book may sound like a new business venture, but actually it is the shortest way I could think of saying there is no limit to the variety of designs possible with flowers and plant material. I know that everyone who is interested in the art of arranging flowers finds the creation of new design a constant challenge. For design, as we all know, is the basic quality in all good floral art. How to come upon variation of design with flowers and plants is the first consideration for both the novice and the expert artist with flowers.

Many years ago when I was preparing to teach a class of novices in the art of arranging flowers, I found a splendid book on design in the public library. This was before many books had been written on the subject of flower arranging, and I was trying to find some way to start my class that would be encouraging to the women beginning. So often I had found that women start the study of an art—the art of flower arranging particularly—and imagine it will be just a fun thing that will require very little thought or effort. When the teacher starts immediately by telling them about design theory and uses any technical terminology, they often get frightened and do not show up for the second lesson. The following lines from a book by Ernest A. Batchelder, *Design in Theory and Practice*, proved most helpful to me and seemed to sound the right note of encouragement to my beginning pupils. I cite them here with the hope that they may have the same effect upon you. *"Let us give emphasis to one point at the start. The ability to design is not a secret that nature has vouch-safed to genius alone. It is quite as much a matter of persistent work as fortuitous inheritance. Indeed, there is so much of common sense and orderly thought involved in the process of building up a design that a resignation to failure is often an unconscious admission of one's own lack of persistence and energy."*

So you need not be in the genius class to be a good designer of flowers. As far as persistent work is concerned, I know from many years of teaching experience that some of the most successful pupils I have ever had in design with flowers were those who came with little or no artistic background or, as Mr. Batchelder said, "fortuitous inheritance," but they worked at it persistently, and today some of them are teachers, accredited judges, and all of them are happy with a new means of self-expression.

There is a way of making people feel at home when they begin to learn a new art. I found that emphasizing the close relationship among all of the arts helps to accomplish this attitude. Almost every-one has had some knowledge of the art of musical composition, the dance, painting, interior decorating, landscape designing, and if you cannot reach them in any of these fields, there is always the nice homely art of cooking. So let's start by comparing.

Musical composition and floral design have a very close kinship. The musician has just so many notes with which to compose, each one with a different pitch. By placing these notes together the theme of the musical composition is created. The development of the theme, the melody, the rhythm, and the harmony, with all the pos-sible variations, produces the musical design. How beautiful the music is depends on whether all the elements of good musical com-position are present and whether the combination of notes to pro-duce the theme has "ear" appeal.

The *dance* is an art form, one of the oldest art forms in the history of mankind. The choreographer is the designer. The dance steps are patterns that are linked together in rhythmical sequences. The bodies of the dancers take on curves and angles of interesting and beautiful lines.

No one will argue when you say that *painting* and *drawing* are arts related to designing with flowers. Often the flower artist describes his art as "painting with plant material." The thing that always amazes me is that the average artist working with oils or water color as the medium rarely arranges flowers to paint so that they have any design when he puts them in a vase. The old Dutch and Flemish masters, in some of their most famous floral paintings, instinctively gave their floral compositions good design. They were usually massive arrangements of flowers of many forms and colors. Designing or composing the canvas, laying out the forms with black lines on white canvas or blocking it in with color, presents the same consideration of the elements and principles of design considered important in designing with flowers. In the handbook of the National Council of State Garden Clubs the elements of design, as employed in the artistic arrangement of cut plant material, dried or fresh, are defined as "COLOR, LINE, FORM, PATTERN, TEXTURE." The principles of design are listed as "BALANCE, DOMINANCE, CONTRAST, RHYTHM, PROPORTION, SCALE." Different books on the subject of design by well-known artists may differ a little with these definitions, but fundamentally they all have the same end in view and prove the close relationship of design to any of the fields of art.

Interior decorating might really be called interior designing. Each article of furnishing, which includes the carpets or floor coverings as well as the window treatments, creates a design with the walls of the room framing it. The color combinations, furniture forms, and accessories placed in the room give it balance, proportion, line, rhythm, color harmony, and form that make up the elements of color design found in a flower arrangement of merit or any other art form. I could never understand how or why some of our top interior decorators are such poor flower arrangers. I am beginning to feel that it is because they have always felt that being able to arrange flowers is instinctive and requires no special training. If they would apply the same principles of design and know-how with color that they use in their interiors, they would be masters in the art of designing with flowers.

Landscape designers often compare their work with that of the flower arranger. They relate the form of their garden to the shape of the house, the line of the path, the height and breadth of the tree or shrub, as a part of the whole design. For foundation planting, the house is the focal point. In the garden a figure, a bench, a large rock, a pool, or a garden gate may be the object from which the lines of the garden design flow. These are comparable to the lines of the flower arrangement and are designed to come together as an axis or terminus to form the focal point.

You'll probably ask, "And how does the cook find a relationship between the art of *cooking* and the art of designing with flowers?" Compare the variations of taste and the elements that create the variations in cooking with the lines created by branches and flowers of a flower arrangement. The master recipe is comparable to the main lines of a floral design. Variations of the master recipe with additions or omissions of certain taste elements create a variety of dishes that are appealing to the eye and the palate. Cooking is surely an art comparable to all others. If more people thought of cooking as an art, there would be many happier cooks and the food would be more beautiful to the taste.

So let us feel at home with the art of designing with plants and flowers. Approach the subject of design in this medium as you would the study of design in any of the aforementioned arts. You would not expect to know all about musical composition in five easy lessons, nor would you expect to understand all there is to know about painting without many lessons and lots of practice. Therefore, do not be discouraged if you are not an expert flower designer after you read a few books and enter a few flower shows. Have no feeling of inferiority because you are not able to create beautiful designs with flowers instinctively. This is an art that requires study and practice, but one that repays the student artist threefold for the amount of time, study, and energy expended.

1

Floral Designs
Take Form

There are such wonderful possibilities for variety of design with flowers and plants. It seems a pity that more "artists with flowers" do not take advantage of them. After a great deal of thought and study I have found many books, teachers, and lecturers assume that students know much more than they really do about this subject. High-sounding phraseology and terms that are unfamiliar to the un-initiated make the subject seem much more difficult than it really is.

I remember how lost I felt when I first listened to speakers talk about the art of designing with flowers, or flower arranging, as it was most commonly known. I often look back and think how fortunate I was in the beginning to have won the number of awards I did. My information on this subject was so sketchy. My passionate love for all growing things and the study of art in my youth came to my rescue when I was invited to teach a large group of people from my garden club. I read every book on Japanese flower arranging I could find in the library, and I went back to the books on "design" I had read in school. The facts about design in relation to painting, I found, applied to the art of designing with flowers just as well.

A background that includes some art training is helpful but not essential. There is nothing superficial about the study of "design with flowers." The more thought and study given to the plan, the more interesting the result. If you already know the elements of design, so much the better; but if you do not, perhaps you will be as fascinated as I was to learn that the same elements of design present in the architecture of a building are also present in a design made with plant material. These elements are Form, Pattern, Line, Texture, and Color. They should not be confused with the principles or standards set for design perfection. The elements are always there, just as the chemical elements hydrogen and oxygen are always present in water.

The next time you go to a museum or art gallery or view any piece of design, analyze it and see if it does not have form, pattern, texture, and color.

Some students get the words "form" and "pattern" confused. Frequently the word "line" is confused with "pattern." The following are rather simple definitions that may untangle the confusion.

FORM is the term used to describe the shape of the whole design. The basic forms are the sphere, the cube, the rectangle, the cone, the spiral, the rod, the prism, and the strip. (Fig. 1.)

PATTERN is the term given to the skeleton of the design that fits within the form. The best example of this is the vein in a leaf.

LINE is the term used to describe the visual path the designer wishes the observer's eye to follow when viewing the design. There is "line" in arrangements made with large masses of plant material as well as in patterns made with a few flowers. (Fig. 2.)

TEXTURE is the surface characteristic of the plant material, container, and accessories used in a floral composition. The "texture" can be described as smooth, rough, dull, shiny, velvety, or sleek.

COLOR may be analyzed as the element that breathes life into the design. If the pattern is the skeleton, then color is the "flesh and blood."

Color gives drama to a design with flowers. The artist may use the color in the flowers or foliage as he would pigment in an oil painting. The "line" may be defined in the pattern by use of strong color against weaker values. For example, a mass arrangement of yellow gladioli and yellow snapdragons has a beautiful pattern, but the "color" of orange and red dahlias arranged against it would produce the "line."

Color may give the design balance, for it has visual weight. The

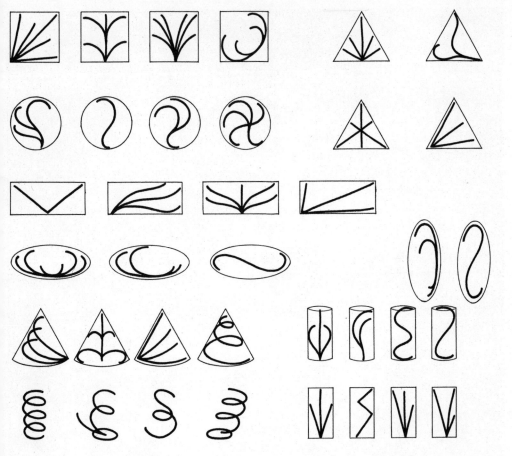

Figure 1 *The basic forms are the sphere, cube, rectangle, cone, spiral, rod, prism, and strip.*

most subtle use of color is often the most effective. We will discuss color again in a later chapter. (Plate 1.)

The key to planning a variety of designs depends upon how you handle your knowledge of these elements. It does not matter how you begin to plan—whether you start with the form and draw your pattern within it or whether you start with a pattern that may have been inspired by an interesting bend of a branch or stem. You may start with a beautiful color harmony of flowers and foliages. The related textures or contrast of textures of flowers, flower receptacle, or accessories may also be the starting point for the idea for your design. For example, I have a collection of shells that have inspired me because of their wonderful textures, color, and form. I use them as receptacles and accessories for floral designs and they have inspired many prize-winning arrangements.

Figure 2 Line in arrangements may be achieved with large masses of plant material or with few flowers. Pussy willows, snapdragons, freesia, tulips, green-and-white caladium leaves, and anemones in a white alabaster compote illustrate line in a mass arrangement.

The receptacle is often the starting point from which the designer takes his cue. We shall discuss in another chapter the many kinds of flower receptacles and how they influence the design.

Let us suppose that the artist is looking for an idea for a new design. How to start is the problem. Putting ideas together in an orderly manner is one of the essentials for success. I find I can get organized best by putting my thoughts on paper. When I am working for a lecture and demonstration I am influenced, of course, by the type of design the title of the program calls for. If it is a demonstration of designs for the dining table, my pattern immediately takes on a certain form that will allow for the shape of the table. This is actually a design within a design. I block the forms out on paper. A round form may be pleasing on a rectangular table, or a square form may be pleasing on a round table. I plan the pattern and then start thinking of the receptacle for the flowers. If fruits and flowers are to be used, or fruits alone, the form-color-texture relationship of these parts must be considered. My whole idea may be influenced by finding an unusual piece of foliage. The form, color, texture, and appropriateness of this foliage may influence the entire design.

For example, three rosettes of echeveria, the interesting South African succulent, once were the root for the creation of a completely new idea for a dinner-table design. (Plate 18.) The echeveria has a fleshy leaf, is celedon-green in color, and often has a rosy tinge around the edge of the outer petals. The soft rose color is exactly right with the color of Tokay grapes. More important, the grapes and the leaves of the echeveria had the same textural quality. I did not own an appropriate receptacle or base on which to place this design of fruits and foliage, so I bought a piece of heavy frosted glass cut in an oblong shape, placed two large bunches of grapes in an S-curve pattern within the rectangular form, and used the echeveria to create the "line" and focal point. An interesting effect was obtained by tinting the underside of the glass with rose oil paint rubbed on by hand. The whole effect was very elegant. The idea started with a piece of foliage. (Plate 18.)

It is often better to start with a fresh idea. Sketch the basic form, then the pattern on paper. List flowers that will fit the idea in color, texture, and form, then select flower receptacles to complete the design. A fresh combination of lines to create a pattern may be the spark for your imagination. This happens to me quite often. The

Figure 3 *Spherical line arrangement is composed of ceramic ballerinas and a round bowl of the same glaze with whitened Scotch broom, white snapdragons, white stock, white freesia, and bright red anemones against a red satin background.*

illustration in Figure 3 came about in this way. Ballet was the subject. The sphere was the form that was the nucleus for the idea. This arrangement was made for the International Flower Show and was considered an interpretive arrangement. The ballerinas and the dish in which the floral arrangement was made were designed especially for this exhibition. The "pattern" was created by the whitened Scotch broom and the "line" by the freesias and anemones.

The sphere is the basic form from which many variations of the crescent are patterned. The design in Figure 4 started with the naturally curved branch of high-bush blueberry with the green fruit just turning color. The fruit of the blueberry and the rosy caste of the echeveria at the edge of the petals gave the design the color element. The textures were harmonious also.

Just for the sake of variety, for home pleasure, Figure 5, the "diamond" pattern, was made. The form from which it originated was the square. The equality of balance on each side of the imaginary line that may be drawn through the center would describe it as a symmetrical arrangement. Iris foliage and blue and rose hydrangea clusters made this a simple but not too usual design. In July our gardens in New York State have very little in bloom. The hydrangea shrub is a welcome note of color at this time.

I suppose it's perfectly natural for us to think that in California and Florida there are more dramatic possibilities with the handsome foliages and profusion of blooms that grow there for a much longer season than in the Northeast. I have found, however, that the problems are very much the same there as they are here. The foliages we consider so exotic and wonderful to design with are "old crow" there. It was a real challenge for me to take the most common plant material in Florida and try to do something of distinction with the design. Figure 6 is an arrangement of sansevieria, clipped roadside palmetto palm, and double yellow hibiscus. The copper receptacle with the evenly fluted texture inspired this triangular pattern. The texture of the clipped palmetto cut in round forms harmonizes with the receptacle. The double yellow hibiscus creates the "line" within the "pattern." The form in this case would be the cone.

White wisteria, which grows over my front door, suggested an oval pattern that I completed with double white peony-flowering tulips. The "oval" composition was completed with the white Chinese porcelain figurine. (Fig. 7.)

Figure 4   A crescent form is illustrated in this arrangement of high-bush blueberry and echeveria on frosted glass elevated on a teakwood stand.

Figure 5 Arrangement of iris foliage, blue and rose hydrangea, and hosta leaves in a gray-blue oblong Chinese pottery dish on a teakwood stand makes a triangle or diamond form.

Figure 6 An *asymmetrical triangle form is achieved with sansevieria (snake plant), trimmed palmetto, and double yellow hibiscus arranged in a square, fluted burnished copper container.*

Figure 7   *An oval form is illustrated with white
wisteria and double white peony-flowering tulips
arranged in an antique bronze Japanese usabata
on a teakwood stand. The white porcelain figure
completes the composition.*

Figure 8 *The S-curve, or free form, a pattern within a rectangle, is accomplished with silver moon climbing rosebuds, foliage, and full-blown flowers.*

Modern design had made us conscious of the "free form" design. In Figure 8 the Silver Moon climbing rose has been designed in an S-curve pattern within the "free form." Actually, if we became analytical, the "free form" base in this case had its origin within the rectangle.

In Figure 9 the nautilus shell suggested the "form" and "pattern" of this design with the chinaberry vine, whose leaves are streaked with white, assuming the "line" of the "crescent." The "textural" element plays an important part in bringing an unusual quality to this design. It is not often that the receptacle has an iridescent quality to match that of the blossom placed in it. Here

Figure 9 *(It is not often that the receptacle has an iridescent quality to match that of the blossom placed in it.) Single white dahlias have the same texture and iridescent quality as the pearl nautilus shell in which they are arranged with turquoise berry vine.*

the petals of the small white single dahlia are perfectly related in texture and color to the pearl-like quality of the shell. A white rose or small white tulips would be equally beautiful in place of the dahlias. Ranunculus, tristis, and freesias have been used with equal effectiveness.

An awareness of the elements of design can be such an eye-opener that it not only makes the art of design with flowers come alive, but may deepen the understanding and appreciation of design everywhere.

Plate 1   *Line and balance are created by color in
this arrangement of apple blossoms, rose-and-
white Darwin tulips, rose parrot tulips, and violet-
red parrot tulips in a pewter chalice.*

Plate 2 *An asymmetrical arrangement often depends on visual balance. The design made of Scotch broom, kitten tails (Synthyris), and white dahlias in a black lucite boat-shaped dish is an example.*

Plate 3 When the identical number of lines, forms, and colors are placed on either side of an imaginary line drawn through the center of a floral design, a balance is created that is described as symmetrical. Yellow calla lilies and foliage complementing the sculpture "In Prayer" by Alice Gross illustrate this balance.

Plate 4 There is very little limitation on the color and textures of plant material suitable for design in pottery—as illustrated by this spring garden arrangement of apple blossoms, forsythia, narcissus, Dutch hyacinths, grape hyacinths, and pansies.

Plate 5 *The gamut of yellow and orange-yellow, orange-red, and red-orange flowers available from early spring until late fall are beautifully related to copper in color and texture. Here manzanita, gladioli, tritoma, chrysanthemums, zinnias, marigolds, croton foliage are arranged in a large antique copper dish.*

2

Principles of Design or Design Perfection

The designer strives for perfection in the construction of his design. He may do this subconsciously or deliberately. The genius does not stop to analyze before creating his design. But how many of us can place ourselves in the genius category? It helps a great deal for a set of standards to be written so that the designer, especially the beginner, may judge his own work. It has been agreed by many artists that, to be considered good or better than good, a design made with plant material and flowers must have the following qualifications: BALANCE, PROPORTION, SCALE, CONTRAST, DOMINANCE, REPETITION, and RHYTHM. These seem like a lot of words until you start studying their meaning.

BALANCE

Balance means only one thing when applied to arranging flowers. It means the visual or actual weight of the plant material equally balanced on either side of an imaginary line drawn through the center of the design. (Figs. 1 and 2.) Frequently when the arrangement of flowers is complemented by a stand or table, an accessory or frame, like a niche, the imaginary line is drawn through

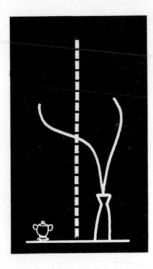

Figure 10   *To determine balance when arranging flowers for a table in the home, draw an imaginary line through the center of the table. The flower arrangement is only one unit of the whole composition.*

Figure 11

the center of the entire composition to test the balance. (Fig. 10.) In a single arrangement of flowers a safe way to be sure of a balanced design is to place the main line of the design (the longest stem or branch) with its tip directly over the center of the composition. If this is impossible to achieve, a balance can be attained by using a large flower, fruit, or foliage form to attract the eye because of its visual weight. Color of strong or deep intensity or the use of an accessory may have the same effect. The design that depends on visual balance is called an *asymmetrical* arrangement. A design can be balanced and placed in a horizontal position. A design can have balance and the main line may be placed in a diagonal position. (Plate 2.) When the identical number of lines, forms, and colors are placed on either side of an imaginary line drawn through the center of a floral design, a balance is created that is described as *symmetrical*. (Plate 3.) It is not difficult for you to judge your design for balance because balance is so easily seen and felt.

This may be a good place to mention some of the ways that designs with flowers and plants fail to achieve balance. A design of plant material is unbalanced when it is top-heavy. This is a common fault found in the work of the novice because it is difficult to sacrifice the length of a stem. (Fig. 11.) The large forms should be placed low in the arrangement, so that they balance the design and give it stability. A safe bit of information to remember is that the small forms are best placed at the outer edge of the design, with a gradual transition of form and color to the axis, or focal point, where the

lines of the design come together. Balance can be created or de-
stroyed by the manner in which color is handled. Color has weight
visually. The light values are light in visual weight and the hues of
dark and strong value weigh heavy visually. (Fig. 12.) To achieve
balance without making a symmetrical design with actual equality
of balance is an artistic accomplishment. Frequently an asymmetrical design has the most style. Like the manner in which a man's
or woman's hat is designed and worn, an asymmetrical balance
created by an angle may make it a work of art or just another head
cover. (Plate 2.)

PROPORTION

The terms "proportion" and "balance" are often used together in
describing design with plants and flowers. It is seldom that a design
with flowers or plants can be isolated from its container or base.
Even the background—whether it is home or exhibition hall—must
be taken into consideration when making a selection for a well-
proportioned design. (Fig. 13.) There used to be a few cut-and-
dried rules, including one about the main line of the arrangement
never being more than one and a half times the width of the flat
dish or height of the vase. These are still good proportions to guide
the beginner. We have progressed in these past twenty or thirty
years and have learned that a design may be two or three times the
width of the dish or the height of the vase, depending on the background, the position (height of table, size of niche, size of wall
space), or whether the arrangement is to be viewed above or below
eye level. Some perfectly beautiful and distinctive designs with flowers have been given no recognition in flower-show competitions because the judges were still using the old rules. Like all the fine arts,
it is most difficult to judge art with flowers by a hard-and-fast set of
rules and measures.

SCALE

Years ago when the horticultural perfection of a bloom and its
length of stem was what counted most in judging its beauty, it was
not uncommon to see extremely long-stemmed flowers (roses, for
example) with relatively small blooms placed in very tall vases.
There was no design intended. The flowers were displayed for their

Figure 12 *Victorian mass arrangement designed for the International Flower Show in New York City portrays with flowers the play* Victoria Regina. *White snapdragons, lavender and white lilacs, white freesia, pink roses, blue daisies, white calla lilies, and deep-purple violets are appropriately arranged in a white alabaster compote complemented by a white alabaster British lion on royal-purple velvet. The use of small forms of deep color clustered together helps to create balance.*

Figure 13   *Proportion and balance are illustrated by an arrangement of yellow-green azalea branches and pale pink peonies in an olive-green Chinese pottery vase.*

horticultural perfection. Length of stem meant quality. Today all professional florists are conscious of design with flowers and they know that flowers should be arranged so that the flowers, vase, and background are in perfect scale. Scale may be described as one of the principles of design that considers the relationship of the size of all the component parts of a design. If the flowers are small, no matter how long the stems, they should be cut down in scale according to the size of the vase. Miniature arrangements are greatly admired because of the careful workmanship of the designer in spite of the minute size of the design parts. It is not enough to cut the stems short and place them in a small vase, however. The flowers and foliage must be in scale with the vase as well. (Fig. 14.)

There is no actual rule to guide the designer in selecting an accessory to complement the floral design. An object used to complete the design other than the plant material should not dominate the picture. It should not be too small in relation to the size of the arrangement. Like the selection of the vase, the accessory must be in scale with the plant material and flower receptacle.

CONTRAST

Contrast is a design principle that is often present when plant material and flowers combine variety of texture, color, and line to create interesting effect. A flower arrangement may have all the design elements present, may be well balanced, proportioned, and scaled, but still make no artistic contribution. There are many ways of achieving distinction in design. One of the most obvious is to become aware of the value of contrasts in design parts. If you analyze a design that has glamour, you often find that it is the artist's ingenious use of contrasts that has given the art drama. A leaf of strong color and coarse texture may be combined with a bloom of smooth silken texture to make just the right contrast. (Fig. 15.) Designing calla lilies in a wood chopping bowl may make a more dramatic textural contrast than arranging them in pottery. The study of contrast as a required principle of good design with plants is both fascinating and provocative. (Fig. 16.)

DOMINANCE

Another way the designer with plant material can keep his art fresh, alive, and original is in his or her selection of the dominant

Figure 14 *Flowers and foliage must be in scale. Miniature shell arranged with minute sprays of heather and oxalis blossoms and buds is an example.*

note in the design. Dominance is a quality to be understood and used in creating designs with flowers. With no dominant color or form, the design may be flat, monotonous. The focal point or point of interest in a floral design often is the part of the design where the dominant color or form is found. This part of the arrangement, often termed the "axis," is where all the lines either visually or actually come together. Here a cluster of small blooms of vivid hue may be clustered together to give the necessary accent. This is where the eye is often focused on a large and imposing textured or unusual form of foliage or seed pod. This is no accident. The artist intentionally arranges the design parts so that there is a dominant note. A bloom may be made dominant in focus and color by placing a leaf

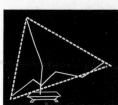

Figure 15 *A leaf of strong color and coarse tex-*
ture may be combined with a smooth silken
texture to make just the right contrast. Salmon-
pink poppies, buds and seed pods arranged with
rhubarb foliage in a green Chinese pottery dish
illustrate this contrast.

in back of it. This is done very much as the artist designs with paint. A stroke of umber or violet pigment around and in back of a bloom makes it come forward on the canvas—a trick that gives the bloom third-dimensional quality. This same effect may be achieved with a leaf or blossom in designing with flowers.

Some years ago when I was an inexperienced flower arranger I exhibited an arrangement of flowers for a bridal luncheon table at the exciting International Flower Show in New York City. We were permitted to stand behind a roped-off area and hear the judges' comments. I had used white lilac, white freesia, white tulips, and

Figure 16 *Calla lilies designed in a wooden chopping bowl may make a more dramatic contrast than pottery or glass. Whenever possible, use calla foliage and buds with the blossom.*

some lavender lace flowers and a few purple pansies to complete the theme. I used the white lilac to represent the sails of a boat, developing the design further with transcending forms of freesia, buds, and full-blown white tulips. This was an all-white arrangement, and my training in painting made me feel the need of using shadows of lavender and purple between and behind the forms I wished to dominate the picture. The judges apparently did not understand my intention. One said to the other, "You know, this arrangement isn't bad, but that introduction of lavender and purple in a bridal arrangement makes me feel that the bride must be getting on in years."

I often remember Mr. John Taylor Arms, president of the American Etchers' Society, when he lectured to the garden clubs and said that the voids in a design with flowers were as important as the lines. Ever since then I unconsciously examine the spaces the lines form. Frequently distinction is brought to a design with flowers by the clever uneven patterns that the voids create to dominate the design. (Fig. 17.)

RHYTHM AND REPETITION

To those who have always considered the word "rhythm" descriptive of the beat of music or steps in the dance, the idea that designs with flowers have rhythm may seem a new one. When you learn to analyze a design for perfection, you will see what an important principle this is. The designer with flowers controls the viewer's eye, absorbing the beauty of the design by the rhythmical manner in which he places the elements of color, form, and line so that the eye passes in gradual steps from one color and form to the next with a repetition of rhythm sequence as obvious as if it were beaten out on a drum. The clever transition of small forms, uneven forms, lines, and colors creates many varieties of rhythm in design. (Fig. 18.)

Some students in the art of design with flowers mistakenly believe that the only arrangements of flowers that have rhythm are those with swinging, curved lines that wing into an S-curve or twirl around in a circular form of design. Actually, a flower arrangement may be a perfect rhythmic design in itself and be composed entirely of straight lines. (Fig. 18.) Sometimes the design depends on accessories placed near it to complete the rhythm. (Fig. 19.)

Figure 17 *The uneven pattern created by the voids brings distinction to a spiral design of palm foliage and amaryllis blossoms in a black metal container.*

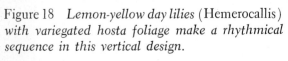

Figure 18   *Lemon-yellow day lilies* (Hemerocallis)
with variegated hosta foliage make a rhythmical
sequence in this vertical design.

Figure 19 *The author's blue-ribbon arrangement at the International Flower Show in New York illustrates rhythm with a ceramic Balinese dancing figure, leucothoë, bronze snapdragons, and orange clivia in an antique bronze Chinese vase.*

A flower design may be made to complement another art form, like a painting or a piece of sculpture. The design with flowers or plants then becomes a unit in an artistic composition. To use flowers for the home so that they do most to enhance the beauty of a room's design, the placement of the furniture and the accessories should create a rhythmical pattern. When the eye jumps from form to form and color to color without a gradual repetition of pattern and color, there is no design. Learning to feel the rhythmic beat of color and form in design with flowers is a stimulating experience.

Rules and regulations have been written to try to satisfy the need for guidance for those studying to be artists with flowers. Lou Tsai Che, Chinese teacher and philosopher, wrote: *"Some say it is excellent to have a method and that it is bad not to have one, but to rest content with a method alone is worse still. One should at first observe rules rigidly, then make them subservient to one's own intelligence. The great object of possessing a method is to be able to demonstrate finally one acts independently of method."*

The true artist must never be stifled by too many restrictions. Often those who are too easily satisfied with their efforts are the ones who need to use the yardstick of perfection in testing their work. The true artist is never completely content with his art, but with each new design hopes to create a composition more beautiful than the one before. Learning the principles of design simply means knowing the standards by which your art is judged so that you may be the better judge of it yourself.

3

The Flower Receptacle Influences the Design

The manner in which an idea with flowers is conceived varies with the individual designer. To some a blossom, the bend and curve of a branch, or the texture and color of a leaf may be the beginning of an idea. More often, however, the design is inspired by a more permanent part of the designer's equipment—the flower receptacle or container, as it is generally called. It is no wonder that beginners in this art are confused. There is such a great variety of receptacles obtainable today that selection is very difficult.

Designers are interested in flower containers for two purposes: for home decoration and for exhibition. When a vase is selected for home use it is given the same consideration as the selection of a lamp or picture. Its position in the room, the color scheme, relationship to style and period of furniture—all must be taken into consideration. Textures of fabrics and wood, as well as the relationship between the flower container and other pieces of bric-a-brac, must also be thought of. Of course the selection need not be limited to only one suitable container for one particular spot in the room. The vase may vary with the varieties of design suggested by different kinds of plant materials at different seasons of the year. A container that is a perfect accessory to the home and is so pliable it takes on a new look every time a fresh arrangement of flowers is placed in it is the designer's treasure. This chapter is intended to help you recognize and appreciate it when you see it.

The artist interested in exhibition at a flower show selects the container after much deliberation, knowing that if the competition is keen a receptacle that is particularly appropriate may help win the blue ribbon. It sometimes takes weeks to find just the right vase. It must be one in good proportion to the space allotted to the exhibitor. Filling the space is very much like blocking out a composition on canvas. The size of the canvas dictates the scale and proportion of the objects the artist puts down in the design. The relationship between color and texture of the plant material should be so harmonious that there is no apparent division between the container and its content. Even if the edge of the receptacle is not covered with foliage, the eye should flow from receptacle to plant material without stopping. The shape of the container and the form of the design must be one to create the most beautiful effect. If this is true, then the basic forms for floral design that were discussed in an earlier chapter—sphere, square, rectangle, triangle, and oval—are good basic shapes to look for in selecting a container. The shapes are good when they stand vertically or when they stand in a horizontal position. It is not advisable to consider color alone when combining flowers, plants, and containers artistically. Color relationship is important, but textural relationship gives the artistic effort greater subtlety.

POTTERY, PORCELAIN, CHINA

There is a vast assortment of pottery receptacles from which the flower designer may choose. Every part of the world has its own ceramic clays, styles of design, and glazes. There is no limit to the variety of textures, patterns, and colors to inspire the artist. (Fig. 20.)

When I was first studying the art of designing with flowers I was so frustrated by the lack of receptacles in good simple forms and solid color glazes that I started making my own ceramic containers. It was an interesting experience, and although my pottery had a definite "handmade" look it also gave my designs a distinctive quality. (Plate 4.) Generally speaking, there is very little limitation in the colors and textures of plant material arranged in pottery.

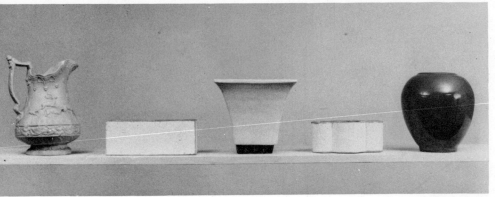

Figure 20 *There is a vast assortment of receptacles for the flower designer to choose from.*

Naturally the heavy, thick, coarse textures look best with bold dramatic flowers and foliages.

The formula for a fine clay imported from China many years ago is still used in the manufacture of porcelain and china dishes and vases. The fine translucent quality of this porcelain suggests the use of delicate flowers with that same translucent texture. Roses, lily of the valley, sweet peas—in fact, any of the flowers that you would consider delicate enough to design in thin Venetian glass— are appropriately arranged in porcelain and china.

COPPER

Copper is a very popular metal used for flower containers. Wonderful textures and colors are obtained in this metal by the way it is annealed and finished. With an assortment of copper dishes and vases the flower designer can have a large variety of textures

Figure 21 *Copper is a very popular metal for flower containers.*

and colors well related to almost any plant and flower. Copper may be sleek and smooth, rough and earthy-looking, or washed with pewter and fluted. It may be orange-red and shiny or oxidized with a bluish-violet cast. It can look like bronze with a smooth hard brown finish. Every floral designer who has a few copper receptacles in his collection values them for their versatility. They are a wonderful foil for flowers. (Fig. 21.) When copper is shiny and polished it has a beautiful rosy-orange color, like a sunset. The whole gamut of yellow and orange-yellow, orange-red, and red-orange flowers from early spring until late fall fill the color need for flowers arranged in this handsome metal. (Plate 5.)

Annealing copper, I learned, changes its color. This is the process of heating it over a flame to soften it so that it is easily hammered into shape. To oxidize copper even further, so that it appears like bronze, it may be treated with a solution containing sulphur. One dish I made and treated in this manner is very interesting texturally and has a lot of blue, purple, and green that make it very beautiful as a container for blue and purple flowers. Early lavender iris and deep blue ajuga that has a dark bronze leaf are wonderful in this copper dish.

PEWTER

Pewter is another metal that is fine for flower arranging. It is gray in color and is best with flowers when it is allowed to remain dull. Gray foliages look well arranged in it. Many of the buds and new leaves are most harmonious used as the line material for a flower arrangement made in a pewter receptacle. Pussy willows, mulleins, dusty miller, artemisia, tropical eucalyptus, and many of the South African succulent and desert foliages are beautifully related in texture and color to pewter. (Fig. 22.)

With the relationship of the foliage and the container established, there is a large variety of flowers to choose from that look well arranged in pewter. A shallow dish or a vase of pewter should be part of every flower designer's equipment, for there is no limit to the variety of plant material and flowers that design well in pewter. (Fig. 23.) I remember one year becoming enamored of a pewter plate that an exhibitor showed in one of the flower-show competitions, and when I tried to find a duplicate I realized that this was an antique plate and one very hard to come by. I decided that perhaps I would try to make one myself and, much to my surprise, learned that pewter is not difficult to hammer out. The dish was a great success and I've enjoyed using it for many years. Frequently one finds that it is interesting and instructive to make the flower container to suit the design yourself. The piece has originality and is bound to fill the need of the designer exactly.

Sheet lead, a metal that looks very much like pewter in texture and color, can usually be purchased in a plumbing-supply shop. It is very malleable and can be pushed into all kinds of interesting shapes that hold water and are most attractive with flowers.

SILVER

The question of silver and its usefulness for flower design is often discussed. Years ago when flower arranging was a new art in this country, there were some who thought it best to make a general statement advising flower designers that silver receptacles were not

Figure 22   *Gray artemisia foliage with Cambridge red monarda (bee balm) follows the line of the antique pewter coffee pot in which it is arranged.*

Figure 23 *Pewter is another metal that is fine for flower arranging.*

desirable as flower containers. General rules are frequently a challenge to spirited artists, who do not like being restricted, and before long it was proved that silver can and does serve as a fine flower receptacle, provided it is selected as discriminately as other flower containers. The fault found with silver has been that it reflects and confuses the design. It is often fashioned into very ornate, heavily etched, and deeply flanged receptacles that detract from the floral design, but there are innumerable shapes wrought from silver that are most adaptable to floral arrangement. (Fig. 24.) A satin or semi-glossy finish is the most attractive, and the lines should be simple. Some of the simple designs made by Danish and American silversmiths make beautiful flower containers. The compote, footed fruit bowl, dishes shaped like a shell, oval and rectangular vegetable dishes are also lovely for floral designs and are particularly appropriate for the dinner table. Silver oval soup tureens, champagne coolers, and water goblets are beautiful arranged with flowers.

BRONZE

The Japanese and Chinese consider the flower container as the earth from which the plants and flowers grow, and for this reason make extensive use of bronze. Its brown, earthy color makes it one of the most perfect containers for flowers. In this country, antique Japanese and Chinese flower receptacles are quite rare, but fortunately, with the growing popularity of the art of arranging flowers, some of these Oriental containers are being reproduced

Figure 24   Although silver is not popular with the flower arrangers, there are innumerable shapes wrought from this metal that are attractive for floral design, as shown in the silver shell-shaped compote arranged with climbing roses in a crescent design.

Figure 25 *Bauhinia blossoms (poor man's orchid), native to Florida, in mauve and purple look well arranged in bronze.*

and manufactured for export and are available in the market today. (Fig. 25.)

BRASS

Brass is another metal that helps give variety to design with flowers. Like silver, however, if it is too shiny it may confuse the design of plant material arranged in it. It is very interesting to note the great variations in the designs wrought of brass in the different nations of the world. It is a very popular metal in the Middle and Far East and has been used for receptacles for many hundreds of years in Persia, India, Syria, China, and Japan. The tawny shades of gold and rust flowers found in the fall and spring gardens in the northeastern states are happily arranged in this gold-colored metal. (Plate 6.)

GLASS

The great variety among glass receptacles gives the flower arranger a wonderful assortment of textures and colors that lend a quality to floral designs that no other medium can. (Fig. 26.) The delicate hand-blown glass that has fascinated so many tourists traveling in Italy may suggest designs made with delicate flowers—for example, in Figure 27 the rose or the passionflower and its vine. Possibly the Eucharist lily, sweet peas, nasturtiums, or any other of the delicate and fragile flowers that would be well related to a thin, fragile glass are most appropriately designed in Venetian glass. Mexico is the source of another texture of glass. This glass is not clear, usually has air bubbles in it, and is frequently found in a variety of colors—all of which make it most appropriate for any of the hardy, coarse garden flowers.

Alabaster and milk glass can be used very much like white porcelain or pottery. Simply designed glass from Holland, Sweden, and Denmark makes fine receptacles for floral compositions. Effective use can be made of the interesting textures and shapes of old pressed glass. And contemporary designs made of heavy glass are very usable with bold flowers of strong line and color that suit some of our contemporary interiors.

Contrary to the idea that glass calls for delicate flowers, handsome arrangements can be made in a heavy, clear glass vase with branches

Figure 26 *Glass containers come in a wonderful assortment of textures and colors that lend a quality to designs made of flowers.*

of a budding tree like the horse chestnut. The stems visible under water are a part of the design and should be stripped of all leaves, unless the leaves and extra lines enhance the picture. If mechanical devices are necessary to secure the stems, the mechanics must be hidden. When the stem of the arrangement is visible through clear glass, the entire arrangement need not be as tall. Low glass dishes are no problem at all, and all artists should have an assortment of them. Clear glass takes on the color it is placed on and therefore makes a fine receptacle for flowers on the dinner table, where the color of the table linen shows through. For the beginner, if given a choice of only two flower containers, it would be my suggestion that he select first a footed fruit bowl or compote and, second, a flat, shallow, oblong glass dish. Both of these flower containers are so adaptable to all parts of the home and are so easily made beautiful with designs of flowering material that the novice will find them a fine beginning for his work with floral design. (Plate 7.)

Figure 27 *Violet-blue baptisia arranged with pink tea roses in blue Venetian glass form a delicate design.*

IDEAS OFFERED BY FLOWER CONTAINERS

Ideas do not come easily for everyone. Let us discuss all the possibilities the flower container offers. It is true that flowers can be designed in almost any conceivable receptacle, and in some instances beautiful designs are made without the apparent use of any receptacle to hold water. These designs are made by using a wooden board, straw or bamboo mat, glass, marble, or even a flat tray as the base on which the design is placed. The mechanics that make this type of arrangement easily possible include a small dish with a pinholder secured in it, just big enough to hold water to keep the fresh plant material alive, but small enough to be hidden by the design material itself. This type of container is the answer to "When is a flower container not a flower container?" This really is a base and can be cut in the designer's own pattern. A square, oblong, round, oval, or even free form can be the foundation on which a beautiful design of plants and flowers may be placed. They are not costly and have wonderful adaptability. (Fig. 28.)

Designs with fruits and with fruits and flowers are very easily made on a flat surface. If the board seems too flat for the table on which it is placed, a great variety of stands can be used to elevate it. A small wineglass or low glass candleholder may act as the footing, both of which give a plain piece of frosted glass a very elegant look. If you do decide to design your own base on which to arrange flowers, remember to cut a pattern of paper before taking it to the glazier or to the mill. The position of the container on the base gives the arrangement balance and style. When ceramic art or sculpture is used as an accessory to an arrangement of plant material, a base may give the entire composition unity. If you are fortunate enough to find a shop that sells the lovely teakwood stands and bases imported from the Orient, you will find them a priceless part of an exhibitor's or designer's collection.

The receptacle that was never intended for flowers often helps the artist create interesting effects. An antique coffeepot or teapot, a new ice bucket, candy dishes, soup tureens, gravy boats, sugar bowls, a celery dish, Dad's tobacco humidor or fishing creel can often spark a beautiful idea. Kitchen utensils, too, often fill the bill perfectly. A nice flat piepan, painted just the right color, can

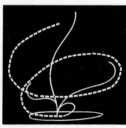

Figure 28 A *board cut from the red cedars of California makes a fine base for an arrangement of angel's-trumpet* (Datura arborea) *with sea grape from Florida's west coast.*

Figure 29　A *natural piece of driftwood and a ceramic figure of Pan playing on his pipes offer the designer a wonderful stimulant for his imagination. This spring arrangement of pussy willows, yellow statice, yellow calendula, yellow mignonette, and green galax leaves was designed for the International Flower Show—Invitation Class.*

look as elegant as an imported bronze from the Orient if placed on a teakwood base.

In addition, Nature's phenomena offer the designer a wonderful stimulation for his imagination. Driftwood, for example (Fig. 29), has become so popular as a designer's tool that beachcombing has become a new occupation and not just a pastime. Shells make wonderful receptacles and accessories for floral designs and have been an inspiration to designers for centuries. Shell shapes have been reproduced beautifully in ceramics, glass, and metals.

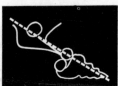

Figure 30 *A sea shell inspired this arrangement of artemisia and coral Ballerina petunias.*

Learning to recognize shells by name and origin is a study in itself. Shells and coral, in all their beautiful formations, are found in the tropics but can be purchased in almost all parts of the world. Their unusual natural forms, textures, and colors make them original accessories of floral compositions. (Fig. 30.)

A challenging class in the flower-show schedule is the one that offers each exhibitor the same container. The varieties of design that can be inspired by the same receptacle are limited only by the designer's imagination and skill.

There are not too many pitfalls in selecting a container for floral design. The container should have good basic form without too many fussy variations. For example, a round dish is a good form in which to arrange flowers, but if it has too many heavy overhanging flanges it loses its grace and its adaptability for floral design. The oval shape is lovely whether it stands on end or lies flat on its side. The rectangle is a basic shape, and the vertical cylinder or shallow dish are equally good. Spheres are lovely for floral arrangements, especially if the flowering material has a round blossom that will relate well in shape to the receptacle. It is interesting to follow the round form of the sphere with branches or blossoms that give it a rhythmical motion.

Pedestal dishes in all shapes are for flowers on the buffet or tea table, for dining, and are equally lovely where the design is enhanced by the added height of the footing. A simple round dish can often be given distinction by placing it on a pedestal. A teakwood stand or even a water goblet turned upside down will often give it the desired effect.

Flower receptacles that are not too ornamented are easier to work with. If there is a design on the vase, it must be a part of the composition. Clean, simple lines are best, especially for the novice designer. There always will be a wonderful group of ingenious people who have the ability and imagination to make something out of nothing. If they happen to be interested in flower arranging too, they can be found creating wonderful receptacles for their floral compositions at practically no cost. If beauty can be born of a tin can and a block of wood with a little paint, so much the better. A simple, inexpensive pottery vase can be painted and rubbed with chalk to make it look as if it had been dug out of an Egyptian tomb. A wooden newel post and a little mahogany stain can create a very elegant vase for a contemporary interior.

4

Color Appeal

It was no accident that you were the belle of the party the time you wore that red dress. Red has been a color that attracts, stimulates, warms, and excites ever since time began. What happens to make color affect us so dramatically? Science tells us that there must be 395,000 vibrations per second for the eye to react to the sight of red. Color is to light what pitch is to sound. All color affects us in varying degrees. Some of the hues excite us, like red. Some hues soothe and cool us, like green. (Plate 8.) Blues and purples have been known to depress, and yellow has the effect of sunshine, a happy color. Each hue, with varying degrees of intensity, affects the optic nerve—in much the same way that notes of music, with varying pitch, vibrate on the ear of the listener.

Science explains further that the color we see is the hue that has not been absorbed by the rays of light that illuminate it. It is almost as if a light filter were used to eliminate all the hues present in a substance except the one Nature wishes us to see. By this theory, if a leaf appears green, it is because the rays of light have absorbed all the other hues in it except green. Green is the surface color that remains for us to see. Science also tells us that all the colors in the spectrum are contained in white light. Tiny drops of moisture

Plate 6 *The tawny shades of gold and rust flowers are happily arranged in brass. Yellow acacia, gladioli, and orange lilies are well related to the boat-shaped container of this gold-colored metal.*

Plate 7 *An arrangement of* Viburnum Carlesii *and blue-violet anemone in a shallow glass dish is adaptable for use in all parts of the home.*

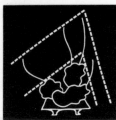

Plate 8   *Some hues soothe and cool, like green. Rhubarb foliage and bells of Ireland in square green oriental pottery dish.*

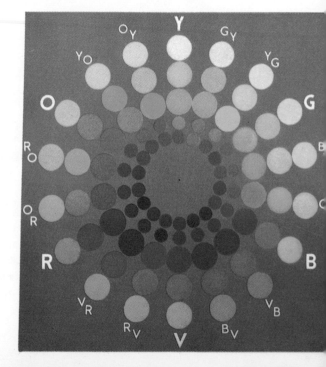

Plate 9   *Homemade color wheel made with coated papers.*

Plate 10   Monochromatic is the term describing
the steps of color from white to black in any hue.
Three values of violet-red snapdragons, chrysanthemums, and stock arranged in a pewter plate
complemented by gray and violet-red rex begonia
foliage illustrate this harmony.

Plate 11 *White flowers are used with those of analogous hues to help relate flowers to the white container. A white alabaster compote is shown with snapdragons of both white and a light value of violet-red, violet-red dahlias, blue-violet ageratum, blue delphinium, and some white feverfew. Analogous hues are closely related on the color wheel.*

that fill the atmosphere are like prisms through which the sun filters. If you have ever watched the light pass through a prism of glass, you know that all the spectral colors are reflected through it, like the rainbow after a shower.

"But what," you ask, "has this to do with designing flowers? With the color already mixed, why should I have to know anything about the theory of color?" The answer is this: Color is one of the most important elements of design. It is such an impelling force that often an arrangement of flowers may not be very impressive in line, form, and texture, but because the color is handled well the design has strong appeal. By the same token, a design with flowers may have an interesting pattern, the forms and textures well placed, but because the artist has used the plant material without color "know-how," the design loses its most important attribute—color appeal.

Even if you are not interested in winning a blue ribbon, a knowledge of color theory can be of great value. It will help you when you select the colors for your wall paint, fabrics for home decoration, clothing accessories, designing your garden, as well as designing with flowers.

COLOR LANGUAGE

Color is described as three-dimensional. These dimensions, like the dimensions of a room (width, length, height) are *hue, value,* and *chroma.*

HUE is the name of the color; i.e., red, violet-red, blue.

VALUE is the amount of light or white, black or lack of light, in a hue.

CHROMA is the degree of intensity of the hue.

When I was a small child I was left quite often in the charge of my mother's younger brother, who was an amateur painter and professional architect. To amuse me he would give me a box of water colors and a brush to play with. He taught me to mix pigment. In this way I learned at an early age how colors are combined to produce other hues. Early practice with color helps to make it seem simple and understandable. But it is never too late to learn about color, and it is not necessary to become involved in scientific theories to do so.

The pigment theory of paint mixing can be understood and remembered if you are willing to take the time to make your own "color wheel." This can be done with water colors, oil paints, or by using coated papers that are manufactured to duplicate the various hues and their values. These coated papers, called "Color Aids," can be purchased from National Council Books, Inc., Box 4298, Philadelphia 44, Pa.

DO-IT-YOURSELF COLOR WHEEL

The hypothesis of the pigment theory is that the colors red, blue, and yellow are the primaries. The theory also is that, having these hues in their deepest intensity, any and all of the spectrum colors may be duplicated by the addition of white and black.

The manner in which the color wheel is constructed is important. Start with a triangle that has equal sides (equilateral). Place yellow at the top point and red and blue at the other two points. Find the center of the triangle by drawing a dotted line from the center of each side of the triangle to the opposite point. (Fig. 31.) Where these dotted lines cross is the exact center. With a compass draw the circle for your color wheel.

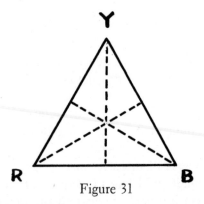

Figure 31

When yellow and blue are mixed, green is the result. Extend the dotted line from the center of the side of the triangle connected by yellow and blue. Place green at this point. Repeat this process, mixing blue and red to create violet, and yellow and red to create orange. These hues are called the secondary colors. The tertiary hues are created by mixing the secondaries with the primaries. For example, the mixture of primary yellow and secondary green may create two possible hues—yellow-green and green-yellow. The last mentioned hue in the hyphenated word is the parent hue. Therefore, this hue would have more of that identified color present in it. Green-yellow contains more yellow than green and is placed closer to yellow on the color wheel. Yellow-green contains more green than yellow and is placed closer to green. This process may be continued around the wheel. (Plate 9.)

VALUE

Each hue in the color wheel may be given a lighter value by the addition of white or a darker value by the addition of black. If you keep adding white to orange-red, it becomes lighter and lighter until it is almost pure white. Actually, the white made from this hue will always be a creamy-peach "off white" because it is derived originally from the hue orange-red. Starting again with the same hue, orange-red, and adding black, going toward the center of the color wheel, the hue becomes darker and darker until it is brown and then black. The black is an "off-black" of a brown caste because the original color from which it was derived was orange-red. I often remember hearing my mother say when she wished to buy either white or black fabric that white and black were the hardest colors to match. I understand now why this is true.

This method of identifying the different values of a hue may be continued in the same manner around the color wheel.

COLOR HARMONIES

In music we learn that when certain notes are combined they form chords that are harmonious. There are musical triads just as there are color triads, and the chromatic scale is one that many of us remember who studied music. Before we can compose with flowers we must learn all the possible harmonious color combinations.

MONOCHROMATIC is the name given to the steps of color from white to black in any hue—or, a simpler description, the tints and shades of one hue. An example would be (light) violet-red snapdragons, (deeper) violet-red chrysanthemums, and (dark) violet-red stock. (Plate 10.)

It is quite difficult to make an arrangement of plant material using the monochromatic values of the same hue accurately. Flowers and plants are already-mixed pigments. Most of them have at least two and sometimes three colors present within their structure. If this color problem is made a part of the flower-show schedule, allowance should be made for the bi-color that exists in most blossoms.

ANALOGOUS harmonies are composed of hues that are closely related on the color wheel and may be combined in any of their values. Analogous hues have the same family name—like yellow, yellow-green, green-yellow, and blue, violet-blue, and violet-red. Snapdragons of both white and a light value of violet-red, violet-red dahlias, blue-violet ageratum, blue delphinium, and some white feverfew illustrate an analogous harmony (Plate 11).

TRIADIC harmonies can be easily identified by the help of the equilateral triangle whose points would fall on the original red, blue, and yellow primary colors. The triads are five colors apart on the color wheel. For example: between yellow and blue there are green-yellow, yellow-green, green, blue-green, green-blue. A lovely triadic harmony is yellow-green, violet-red, red-orange. Yellow-green bells of Ireland, yellow-green coleus foliage, violet anemone, red-orange clivia illustrate this triadic harmony of color. (Plate 12.)

A *TETRAD* is a color harmony formed by combining four hues that are equally distant from each other on the color wheel. See Plate 13 for example.

COMPLEMENTARY harmonies are those hues directly opposite on the color wheel. When these pigments are mixed in equal amounts they produce gray. Again I would remind you that the most beautiful combinations of complementary colors are in the lighter and darker values of the hues rather than in their deepest intensity. A green-blue receptacle with green-blue strelitzia foliage and orange-red Son of Satin dahlia is an illustration of this harmony. (Plate 14.)

A *SPLIT-COMPLEMENTARY* harmony is composed of three analogous hues on the color wheel and the complement of the middle hue. For example: a light value of red-orange gladioli, orange freesia, yellow-orange day lilies, and blue delphinium.

WHAT TO DO ABOUT WHITE FLOWERS

White flowers have great beauty and should be considered for both their color and design. White has all the hues of the spectrum in it. This is often quite apparent in flowers, the live pigment with which we work. There is an iridescent quality present when you examine a white flower at close range. If white blooms are to be used together, consider the different whites as you would shades of any other hue. There are yellow-whites, green-whites, pink-whites, and blue-whites. White flowers look well arranged with foliage that is variegated or that harmonizes with the white. For example, white ornithogalum lilies, which have a lot of yellow-green present in the budded tips, are lovely arranged with yellow-green coleus foliage. White flowers are usually combined with flowers of other hues when the receptacle is white. This relates the container and flowering material. There need not be very much white used to gain the desired effect. (Plate 11.)

COLOR PERFECTS THE DESIGN

Because color is one of the most important elements of design, the principles that are essential to design perfection—*balance, proportion, scale, dominance, contrast*—are present in design with plants and flowers because of the way the pigment is handled.

We mentioned earlier in the chapter that *chroma* describes the intensity of a hue. Hues like yellow, red, and orange cause strong vibration on the optic nerve and appear to come forward in the design when they are used with color of a lesser chroma. Not only does color have chroma (intensity), but it has visual weight in a design. The grayed hues weigh heavier than those of a lighter value. The very intense hues also have visual weight.

If *balance* is one of the principles of design, it can readily be seen how important color is to help the designer achieve balance. Not only are the smaller forms placed at the outer part of the floral design, but the lighter values of color are placed there also. Often small flowers have long stems and flowers of a deep intensity, like small red zinnias or dahlias. This visual weight on the outer part of the design pulls the eye down, and when this happens the arrangement loses balance. The eye should pass gradually from light value, to transitional color groups of a lesser value, to the focal point composed of plant material that is dominant in color and form.

Proportion and balance are linked together in design, because proportionate amounts of color help to create a balanced design. If flowers of one color and value are used together in an arrangement, the flowers of the deeper intensity, because of their visual weight, should be used in quantity and in a position that will give the design stability. When color is not grouped it loses its effectiveness, the eye jumps from hue to hue, and even if the forms are correctly placed the design loses out when scored for perfection.

Equal amounts of color make for a monotonous picture except when the design is intended to be symmetrical, which would demand exact amounts of form and color on either side of the imaginary central line. "In Prayer," by Alice Gross (Plate 3), is the title given the ceramic head complemented by a symmetrical arrangement of yellow calla lilies with their own variegated green-and-white foliage.

DOMINANCE

Experts speak of the "dominant note" as being either present or lacking in design with flowers. Some believe that the note of dominance can be achieved by the use of a large form in the design. Others contend that a sharp contrast of texture will bring a domi-nant quality to the arrangement. There are many ways of achieving dominance. The use of intense color with its vast dramatic possi-bilities, however, seems to me a certain way to get this result. (Plate 12.)

RHYTHM

Some designers believe that the only way to create a rhythmical composition is to find a branch with an interesting curve, or bend a supple twig to create a swinging line. It is true that a curved branch or a manipulated leaf gives the design a feeling of motion, but it is the direction the eye takes through color that creates the illusion of rhythm. The smooth passage of the eye from hue to hue, value to value, combined with the bend and curve of a branch or leaf, creates a rhythmical quality.

CONTRAST

I have seen distinctive designs of plant material that have no sharp contrasts of color or texture. Arrangements can be made that depend on the drama of form, pattern, and line to gain the quality called "contrast." The most obvious way to achieve con-trast in a design with flowers, however, is through use of color.

This is not the only way, but the strong emotional appeal of color and the great variety of contrasting hues make it a natural way.

SCALE

When we discuss scale in relation to color in a design with plant material, we refer to the size of the color units in the design in relation to each other. We cannot discuss the color units in the floral arrangement, however, without considering the size of the color unit the receptacle represents in the design. If a flower design is made for a flower show and a background is furnished, the size and color of this background will influence the relative colors in the design. If the flowering material is designed for home decoration, the size of the color units in the room must be in scale with the other color units in the room. The size of the color unit of the floral design is decided on in much the same manner that the decorator decides on the amounts of accent colors to be used in the sofa cushions or in the fabric in a chair covering. In judging flower arrangements I have often felt like removing an arrangement intact from its container to a much smaller one even when the height proportions were correct, because the color had been used in units too small in relation to the size of the other design parts.

Yes, it was the red dress that helped make you the belle of the party, but it takes a little more than a red dress to hold the attention after the eye has been stimulated by the color. So it is with floral arrangements. A vase filled with flowers and foliages of vibrant hues may draw the eye, but if the design and color are not handled well, attention is soon diverted.

5

Engineering the Design

To have command of the art of designing with plants and flowers you must be somewhat of an inventor, an engineer, and a mechanic. You must be inventive because there is no limit to ideas for design nor is there any rule that dictates the kinds of devices that may be used to make the design stay in place. Each method of "design control" described here was somebody's invention at one time. If you are able to originate a better idea, your method may become every flower designer's tool in a short time. You must be an engineer because before you start to make your design every part of the construction must be planned, and you must be prepared with all the necessary equipment to lay a good foundation for the design structure.

You must be a good mechanic. The viewer should not be made aware of the mechanics used to make the design stay in place. Once put in position, the design must stay together. To accomplish this successfully, you must be deft, precise, and neat. Design with plants and flowers is an orderly art.

EQUIPMENT

The key to an artist's success is often found in the little basket that holds the "engineering" tools of the flower arranger. We take

Figure 32 *Equipment is essential to engineering the design. Needle-point holders, wire, plumber's lead, floral tape, and tubes assist the designer in his work.*

for granted that an artist using oil paints needs good pigment, brushes, and canvas. The artist with flowers needs good tools also. Fine sharp flower shears or small pruning clippers, a small bundle of wire in different gauges, a roll of Scotch tape, green florist's tape, floral sticks, glass or plastic test tubes, plasticine or floral clay, three or four heavy needle-point holders, and you are ready to tackle almost any design problem. (Fig. 32.) Mind you, I said "almost" any problem. A new problem may require an individual piece of equipment that may be needed for the construction of only *one* design. I remember an ingenious holder made of three lengths of one-inch lead pipe soldered together that I had specially made to support the weight of tall, heavy branches designed for a large copper dish.

WHAT MECHANICS CAN DO

The same equipment is not practical for the construction of every design. The form of the design dictates the shape of the vase, the form and color of the plant material, and also the kind of mechanics. If the receptacle is tall and deep, there are different holders to keep the design in position. If the receptacle is shallow, the weight of the plant material and the relative size of the container will determine the kind of holder. If the container is transparent, the holder must be concealed more ingeniously than if the container is opaque.

With good mechanics, short stems with large blooms can be lengthened to fit into the artist's pattern. (Fig. 33.) If a vase is very deep and causes a problem with stem lengths, the stems may be lengthened by wiring an additional stem to them. Just be sure that the stem of the design material reaches water. If a piece of foliage (like coleus, echeveria, croton) has a stem that is too short to reach water, a small vial of water holding the stem may be fastened to a stick with green floral tape so that it cannot be seen. (Figs. 34, 35.) The stick can be cut to any desired length, and the short stem gets the water it needs to remain crisp and fresh in the arrangement. A straight branch can be manipulated so that it bends to enhance the design (Fig. 36) and a stiff leaf can be made to bend into a dramatic curve. (Figs. 37, 38.) A soft, weak stem may be made to appear strong and a soft stem given support. Small flowers of strong or dark value may be held together and the heads of large flowers kept erect.

FLOWER HOLDERS

The pin-cushion type of holder with a heavy lead base and small needle points originated in Japan and is the most popular type for use in a shallow receptacle. It is often necessary to keep the holder from slipping, and this can be done by pressing plasticine (modeling clay) or floral clay to the bottom or sides of the thoroughly dry holder and dish. Small rounded stones, marble chips, glass marbles, sand (white or colored), or crushed glass may be used to hide the needle-point holder in a shallow dish and also help keep it in place.

If you wish to leave the needle-point holder in the receptacle permanently, paraffin wax may be used. The wax should be melted, cooled, and then poured into the dry receptacle. As the paraffin becomes firm the holder may be placed on it gently, until it covers the base but not the needle points. When the dish is transparent, I prefer paraffin to floral clay, as the wax hardens white and conceals the base of the holder. Unless the paraffin is softened with

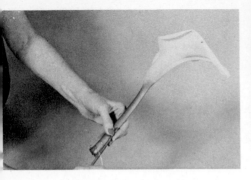

Figure 33 *The floral designer often makes a short-stemmed flower longer by means of a stick with a test tube taped to it.*

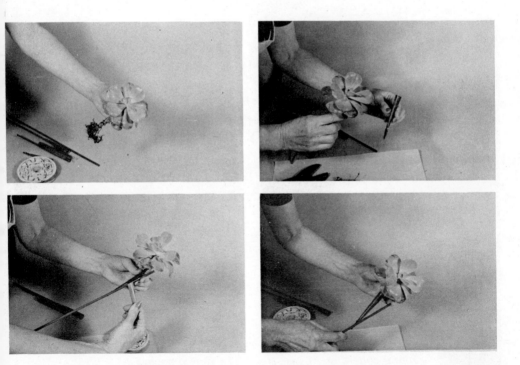

Figure 34 *If a piece of foliage like echeveria has a stem too short to reach water, a small vial of water may be fastened to a stick with green floral tape so that it cannot be seen.*

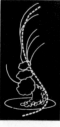

Figure 35   *An arrangement of Russian olive shrub,
echeveria, and blue, green, and red grapes on a
round sphere of frosted glass show how branches
and foliage can be manipulated to form a graceful design.*

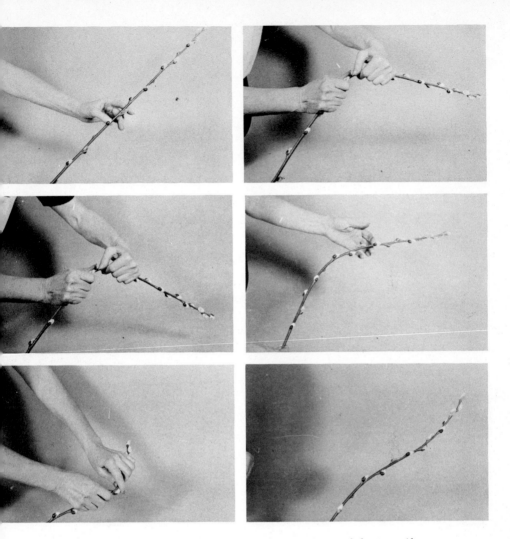

Figure 36 *A branch may be bent into a graceful curve if you know how.*

hot water, the holder is set in the dish for a long time. (Fig. 39.)

Even in a deep receptacle the needle-point holder may be used to secure the main lines of a design. If it is impossible to get your hand inside the container in order to set the holder firmly in place, paraffin may be poured in and the holder lowered into position at the end of a stick and held there until the wax becomes firm.

Even if a receptacle is so deep that it is awkward to work with, do not discard it. The depth problem can be eliminated by pouring sand into the receptacle to the desired height. If sand is too heavy, sawdust or peat moss may be substituted. The holder can then be

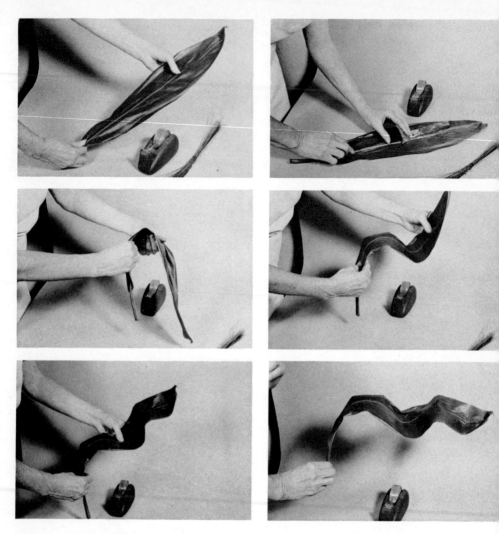

Figure 37 *Wire and Scotch tape secured to the back of a leaf make it possible for the designer to dramatize his design with curving foliage.*

placed on top of the filler and set in place by the use of paraffin, as described earlier.

Crushed chicken wire is quite popular with some flower arrangers. It is usually bunched into a mass and stuffed into a deep receptacle that has a wide opening at the top. The openings in the chicken wire are pushed together to support the stems placed in it. My objection to this type of holder is that soft stems may be broken or bruised when pushed through the crushed wire. Professional

Figure 38 *Designed to illustrate the possibility of creating a mood (anxiety) with flowers, this arrangement of wired brown dracaena leaves, mauve anemone, mauve Scotch heather, and a brown manzanita branch in a blue Chinese pottery dish illustrates the use of wired leaves.*

florists who use this method usually wire flowers in bunches to a stick and push the stick into the chicken wire without injury to the flower stems. The flower stems must reach water, of course.

Oasis is a relatively new plastic substance that professional florists use a great deal because it absorbs water like a sponge and supports the flower stems when wet. Light in weight and clean, it simplifies transportation of arranged flowers in water. Before the manufacture of Oasis the florist used cut fern for this purpose.

Figure 39 *A needle-point holder often slips in the dish if it is not secured. Paraffin, melted, cooled, and poured into the receptacle, will eliminate this problem.*

Figure 40 *Plumber's lead cut in a T-shape is helpful to the designer when the rose is tall and there is no other way to anchor the main stems in place.*

Figure 41 *Japanese flower arrangers have taught us to make holders called kubaris out of wooden sticks.*

Figure 42 *Cut stem under water to revive wilted blossom.*

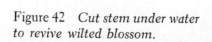

Plate 12   *Triadic harmonies can be easily identified by the help of an equilateral triangle whose points fall on the triads of color as it is moved from hue to hue. An arrangement of yellow-green bells of Ireland, yellow-green coleus foliage, orange-red clivia, and violet-red anemone arranged in an interesting gnarled piece of driftwood form a triadic harmony of color.*

Plate 13   *A tetrad color harmony is formed by combining four hues that are equally distant from each other on the color wheel, as in this arrangement of red-violet anemones, blue grapes, green-yellow branches of witch hazel buds, limes and artichokes, and red-orange gladioli and coleus foliage.*

Plate 14 *Complementary harmony—formed of hues directly opposite on the color wheel—is illustrated in this arrangement of green-blue strelitzia foliage and orange-red Son of Satan dahlias in a green-blue pottery receptacle.*

Plate 15 *A crescent-shaped arrangement may be used in many parts of the home.*

Plate 16 *A simple arrangement of geranium foliage and salmon-pink zinnias in an old pewter teapot are well related in texture and color to the chair and lampshade they complement.*

Plate 17 Fruits may be combined harmoniously
with flowers for the dinner table. White and yellow snapdragons, yellow roses, green grapes, and
croton foliage form a dramatic table decoration
with harmonious accessories.

If the main lines of the floral design are securely placed in a tall vase, the rest of the flowering material may be arranged with relative ease. A holder made of plumber's lead is a good invention for holding flower stems in place and is a practical piece of equipment when it is cut in a "T" shape and proportioned to the size of the material to be arranged. The trunk of the "T" can be hooked over the back of the vase, and the two arms bent to hold the stems or branches in position. (Fig. 40.)

The Japanese have given us some good ideas for homemade flower holders, which they call *kubaris*. The simplest is one made by crossing two branches, each about a half inch in circumference and cut to fit the size of the vase neck tightly so that they cannot slip. The openings formed by the crossed branches act as a support for the main lines of the design. An additional branch crossing in the opposite direction may be used to hold the stems together.

Another *kubari* makes use of a supple branch (rose of Sharon) about three quarters of an inch thick. The branch is cut a little longer than the neck of the vase is wide to allow for a good fit. About one third of the distance from one end, a notch is cut in the wood about an eighth of an inch deep. At the other end, the branch is very carefully split in half up to the notch, and the notched side is bent back. After the plant material is put in position, another piece of wood is used in the small part of the triangle to hold the design in place. (Fig. 41.)

When the designer is working with dried plant material or artificial flowering material, there are two satisfactory kinds of holders. One is a very light sponge-like plastic substance called Styrafoam, and the other is a moist clay that can be bought in a sealed can and hardens rapidly when exposed to air. Styrafoam is so light that it is not always practical to use for large or heavy arrangements. The clay may be formed into a relatively small mass and inserted into any kind of dish or vase, where it adheres and supports the plant material. It becomes rigid and the plant material is permanently fixed in a short time. This clay comes in three-pound tins and can be bought from most suppliers of flower-arrangement equipment.

CONDITIONING FRESH PLANT MATERIAL

If you wish your floral designs to give you a maximum amount of pleasure, fresh plant material must be "conditioned" before it is arranged. This applies especially to flowers cut from the garden or bought freshly cut at a nursery. It is true that some flowers are so hardy that they do not seem to need any special treatment to last well, but generally even these hardy varieties will give longer-lasting beauty to your design if a little extra time is taken to "condition" them.

Conditioning plant material is a simple process—a method of assuring that the plant gets a good drink of water so that it can endure the shock of being cut from the parent plant. Everyone thinks that I have "good luck" in keeping cut plant material, but I know it is not "luck" at all. A plant handled with understanding repays you with the pleasure of its fresh beauty. To be most successful, conditioning should really start with the proper cutting implements. These must be sharp—flower shears, pruning clippers, or knife. A dull implement squeezes the stem and therefore makes it difficult for the stem to absorb all the water it needs.

The best time to cut from the garden is early morning, before the sun is too hot, or late evening. Have a bucket of deep water at hand in a shady part of the garden and place the stems or branches in it immediately after cutting.

Many varieties of plants and flowers need a little special treatment before they are plunged into deep water. Poppies, hollyhocks, poinsettias, and members of the Euphorbia family, for instance, need to have the end of the stem burned before they get a drink. For dahlias, however, the "boiling-water" method comes first. A dahlia specialist taught me to have a pot of water boiling on the stove before going into the garden to cut. The stems are lowered in water while it is boiling and held there for two or three minutes, but care must be taken to keep the heat away from the blossoms. Only an inch or two of the stem need be boiled, then the stem may be placed in deep, cool water.

The next step in the conditioning process for all plants and flowers is extremely important. Place the bucket of water and plant material in a cool, dark place for at least twelve hours before arranging. The stems that were boiled or burned must be treated in this manner again after each pruning. Impaling the stems on a needle-point holder does not seem to break the seal made by the boiling water or flame.

Many years ago I was taught a trick that I have used successfully in reviving flowers and foliages that have seemed completely wilted. It is the method used by Japanese flower arrangers each time they cut a stem. The stem or branch must be placed in a tub or receptacle large enough for both stem and knife to be under water during the cutting. With a sharp instrument the stem is cut at an angle (Fig. 42) and then left in the deep water, without touching the blossoms, for about a half hour. It is amazing how this process will revive a wilted bloom that has suffered because it was arranged in shallow water without being conditioned or because it had to be transported a long distance out of water.

Woody stems should be split at the end for about two inches before being placed in deep water. Hard, pithy stems, like stocks, lupin, or delphinium, should be split at the end or crushed with a hammer. These methods are used so that the stem can get sufficient water.

Sometimes flowers that come from the florist are already conditioned, but I always cut the stems and let them stand in deep water in a cool place, just to be sure. Flowers are often out of water for hours after they have been cut and shipped to market and, even though fresh in the refrigerator, need real conditioning before they are arranged.

Wiring flowers is a technique used by every professional florist. If done with delicacy and precision, it does not injure the flowers and does eliminate the risk of flower arrangements arriving at their destination with the heavy flower heads snapped off. The wire gauge should not be too heavy for the size of the stem, and when the wire is inserted in back of the bloom it can be done with a minimum of injury to the blossom: a quick insertion, pull the wire through, double it down the stem for about three inches, and then, with a twirl of the stem, the remaining long length curls firmly around the stem and wire. After this is done, green floral tape is neatly wrapped around to conceal the wire.

The little glass or plastic vials that are fastened to a stick to allow short-stemmed flowers to reach water must be wrapped with green floral tape. To be sure that this device is not visible in the design, the arranger may find it necessary to wire a stem of foliage to conceal the tube. Wire on a spool is often easier to work with than cut wire and may also be purchased in different gauges.

When the stems are too delicate for wire—violet and nasturtium stems, for example—a spool of green florist's thread is quite useful. Thread may also be used to bind the ends of soft stems like those of hyacinths, amaryllis, and calla lilies, whose fleshy stems split open at the end when impaled on a pin holder in water for a while. It is very disconcerting to make a lovely design with these flowers, believing them to be securely in place, only to find them fallen out of the design a half hour later. A little thread wound around the end of the stem, or thread and a small stick used as a splint, will eliminate this problem.

Whenever possible, it is desirable to use leaves, branches, and stems with their own natural curves. There are times, however, when a stiff leaf can be given a dramatic curl by a neat little trick of wiring the back. This device must not be visible, and with green wire and Scotch tape the method is simple. Place the leaf on a flat surface, then lay the wire on the back of the leaf, close to the vein in the middle. It is not necessary to bring the wire all the way out to the end of the leaf, and it can end just above the stem. With the wire in position, simply tape it to leaf and it's all ready to be shaped. Ti, dracaena, pothos, anthurium, and canna leaves are some of the large varieties that are beautiful when given a permanent wave with wire.

We have all heard the expression "Do not gild the lily." It used to be considered bad taste to dress up a blossom or plant that has natural beauty with unnecessary frills or furbelows. I agree with this idea. I do not like artificial leaf shiners or the use of bows and feathers mixed in with the natural beauty of plants and flowers. However, the use of paint and gilt on leaves, fruits, and dried plant materials is a very practical and decorative idea. Even old, dried arrangements can be attractively transformed by a face-lifting of this kind.

Beautiful ideas for designs with flowers will never become a reality without good engineering. The meticulous work of a good mechanic, combined with a knowledge of design and color, is the "open sesame" to beautiful flower arrangements.

6

Floral Designs for the Home Background

Arranging flowers for the exhibition hall may be an exciting hobby, but most artists using flowers as their pigment consider home their canvas. Decorating the home interior is an art in itself, one easily understood by floral designers. The elements and principles of design applied to the arrangement of a room are the same as those applied to arranging flowers. Form, pattern, line, color, and texture are elements of design found in both arts. BALANCE, PROPORTION, SCALE, DOMINANCE, REPETITION, CONTRAST, and RHYTHM are principles of floral design that are employed also as standards of perfection in room design. Flowers may be just as important to room design as a painting, a lovely lamp, or other furnishings.

Flower arrangements can enhance the beauty of the home in so many ways that they may be called a decorator's instrument. Placed in a plain, unattractive interior, they have the same miraculous effect that a beautiful piece of jewelry has on a plain dress. They give warmth and a lived-in look to an interior that may be perfectly designed but lacking this important quality. No other decoration can give a room the personal touch implicit in flower arrangements. Even a room that has been decorated by a top-notch designer can seem sterile and cold until a living plant or flower is placed in it.

House plants have a more permanent value to room decoration than an arrangement of fresh-cut plant material, but the limitations of the form and color of most potted plants, as well as their temperamental needs for living conditions, make them no substitute for an arrangement of fresh flowers and foliage.

This is probably a good place to mention the usefulness of artificial flowers for floral design. For those who live where there is a short growing season and garden flowers are available only a few months of the year, fresh flowers may be a luxury not everyone can afford. Good reproductions of living flowers may be the answer. Combined with fresh branches and foliages according to the design principles applied to fresh arrangements, the result can be so realistic that the most discerning eye will be fooled. These arrangements are most effective if the varieties of foliage and flower combinations are changed as the seasons change. (Fig. 43.)

Arrangements made of dried foliage, seed pods, and flowers are quite popular for home decoration also. Their sculptural beauty and design possibility make them valuable for permanent decoration. (Fig. 44.) Finding dried material of the right color and texture for your room design requires ingenuity, but even when you are successful, dried arrangements cannot bring the glow of life to the home interior that living plant material can.

A design made of plant material is like a piece of furniture or bric-a-brac. It must be studied for size, shape, color, texture, and general appropriateness in relation to all the other furnishings of the room.

Flower arrangements can perform many visual tricks in decorating the home. Almost every room has a balance problem. If the room must accommodate a large grand piano, an oversized sofa, or a poorly located fireplace, it is difficult to balance. What a temptation to overcome these problems by hiding them behind a vase of flowers. Haven't you seen it many times? A large vase of flowers placed on the grand piano, a huge arrangement standing in front of the fireplace, or an impressive design placed in close proximity to the sofa? This treatment only accentuates the problem. It is hard to believe until you try it how an arrangement of flowers, well proportioned in size and color and placed in another part of the room, can help achieve visual balance.

We have all learned the beauty of line and rhythm that can be created by the artistic handling of color in a flower arrangement.

Figure 43 Artificial flowers are most effective
arranged with fresh foliage. Strelitzia (bird-of-
paradise) is arranged with fresh ti leaves in a
handmade vase by ceramic artist Esther Perry.

Figure 44 *There is a sculptural beauty that adds interest to working with dried material. An interesting piece of manzanita, dried artichoke blossoms, gone to seed and sea-grape leaves combine to make a simple but beautiful design in a bamboo cylinder.*

We know that dark chroma against lighter values come forward in the floral design and that vivid color against a subtle grayed value of its complement produces a striking effect.

In the home, bright notes of color in cushions, chair coverings, pictures, and flower arrangements may be placed to perform the same artistic effect of a rhythmical line of color running through the room. The eye is made to pass from hue to hue by the placement of the colorful objects of decoration. A picture, antique, or any other interesting piece of room furnishing may be highlighted when a flower arrangement is placed near it. The floral design is most effective when it is related to the object it complements. A portrait in an oval frame over the mantel, for example, suggests a crescent-shaped arrangement beneath it, using flowers that pick up the color in the painting. (Plate 15.) Select flowers of lighter and more subtle values of color in the flower arrangement, if you wish the picture to stand out in the room design.

It is much more effective to make a floral design of one hue when it is placed near a chair upholstered in a multicolored fabric. An example of this is the plaid chair and matching lamp shade complemented by a design of geranium foliage and coral-pink zinnias arranged in an old pewter teapot. (Plate 16.) The base of the lamp was an old cider press. Nothing is sacred when a decorator starts looking for lamp bases. Coffee grinders, apothecary jars, a duck decoy, or even an interesting piece of stone may be drafted into use. The same is true of a flower receptacle. The more unusual, the more distinction it may bring the design. It must be related to the room, however, in color, design, texture, and style.

The shape and height of the design are usually determined by the object of furniture it is to be placed on or near. A round table might suggest a spherical design. An S-curve designed in a horizontal position may be lovely on a rectangular coffee table. A tall, narrow wall panel as a background may suggest a slim, vertically designed arrangement. (Fig. 45.)

Flower arrangements in the home are a part of room compositions. Cigarette boxes, ash trays, art objects of all varieties serve as interesting accessories to floral designs. The manner in which you place these objects in relation to the flowers makes for interesting and beautiful effects. (Fig. 46.)

How to make floral designs for a fireplace mantel may pose a problem if the mantelshelf is high. It is advisable to start con-

 Figure 45 *Yellow narcissus with its own foliage designed in a Chinese blue porcelain vase is well suited to a tall narrow wall panel or any other vertical space to be filled in the home.*

Figure 46

structing the arrangement at mantel height and put the finishing touches on it in its final position. If you make the arrangement while seated at a table or even standing before a table of average height, the floral design will look as if it is tipping backward when it is placed on the mantel.

Room comfort, as well as beauty, must be considered when designing flower arrangements for the home. Even a lovely arrangement of flowers is something you would like to push aside if it gets in the way. I remember with amusement an evening I spent squirming from side to side trying to see over, around, and under a beautiful arrangement of flowers that was so large that it was an obstruction between me and my hostess.

DINING ROOM AND TABLE SETTINGS

Except on very special occasions, floral decoration in the dining room is usually confined to the dining table. Of course if you have a dining room where plants or flowers are a necessary part of the decoration at all times, their role in room decoration would be handled very much as they are in the living room. They should be related to the room in color, texture, and style just as a picture for the dining-room wall is. If a corner of the room needs height, this may be an ideal position for a tall pedestal and a vase of dried plant material. Sometimes a few fresh fruits may be added to bring color and interest to the design. (Fig. 47.)

Figure 47 *Fresh fruit may be added to an arrangement of dried material to give it color and interest. Okra seed pods, dried oats, Florida pepper berries, yarrow, and Anaphalis (pearly everlasting) are combined with fresh apples and grapes as a suitable arrangement for the dining room.*

Figure 48 *A pair of compotes arranged with fruits and foliages is one of the simplest to execute. Identical Persian blue compotes with lime-green fruits, andromeda foliage, sansevieria (snake plant), and black grapes will last for a week as decoration in the dining room.*

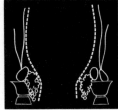

If a picture hangs over the dining-room buffet, a pair of arrangements may be placed beneath to complement it. This can be handled in many ways. A pair of compotes arranged with fruits and foliages is one of the simplest to execute. (Fig. 48.)

Even when the table is not set for dining, it needs some adornment. A lasting and lovely design can be made with branches and fresh foliage. Budding magnolia branches with added pieces of ilex,

Figure 49   Budding magnolia, ilex foliage, andromeda, and brown galax leaves in antique copper or bronze serve as a combination of foliages suitable for the dining table even when it is not set for dinner.

andromeda, and galax leaves may serve as an example. (Fig. 49.) Another suggestion is branches of camellia with andromeda and dark bronze galax leaves.

When the table is set for dining there are many things to be considered. The placement of the crystal, china, and flower arrangement should form a pattern on the table. This pattern can be varied. Often the form of the flower arrangement is suggested by the shape of the dining table. A rectangular table set for an uneven number of guests may be attractively balanced by placing the flower arrangement at one end of the table. Sometimes the table may be set so that everyone has a lovely window view. In this instance the seating is on one side of the table and the flower arrangement is designed horizontally in front of the guests.

A table set for a flower-show competition is judged for over-all *design perfection*. There must be *balance, proportion, scale,* and all the accessories must be *related in texture and color*. Special attention should be given to the height of the water goblets and visual weight of the flower arrangement, as these factors sometimes determine design balance of a table setting. Scale may be determined by the size of the plates, glasses, and table decoration in relation to each other. A table setting is also judged for *harmony of color,* for its *suitability to the occasion, whether it is functional,* and also for the *condition of the flowering material or fruits*.

When setting a table for home or show, you may be interested in point-scoring your own table. A dinner table may be attractive because the colors used are pleasing and harmonious, but if you want to set a blue-ribbon table, remember the accessories must be texturally related. They must be in good scale and in good proportion to the size of the table, and the flower or fruit arrangement should be as a unit of the whole design. Textural relationship is not too difficult to achieve in a table setting. As explained in an earlier chapter, texture is the surface characteristic of the plant material, container, and accessories. It can be described as smooth, rough, dull, shiny, velvety or sleek.

In planning a dinner-table design, it is important to have a nucleus from which your idea evolves. Most often the dinner plate inspires the setting. Sometimes an unusual flower receptacle or special occasion helps to stimulate the imagination. If the dinner plate is very colorful, select one of its hue for the table linen and possibly another for the flower arrangement. It is not necessary to include in

Figure 50 *A spiral design is lovely arranged in a round dish for the dinner table. Pussy willow and tulips in flat round oxidized copper dish.*

the flower arrangement all the colors present in the plate. If a plate of neutral color is used, the flowers and table linen may provide related colors. All the accessories should be related in some way. If you use white plates, for example, you need not use white table linen, but you must relate the plates to some part of the setting. A white receptacle for the centerpiece and a few white flowers in addition to the other colors used may accomplish this for you. Beautiful table settings are much more than just the decoration you make for it.

A popular floral design for the dinner table is a crescent shape. It is easily constructed with a minimum of flowers and foliage and can be viewed from all sides with pleasure. The crescent is particularly suitable for the dinner table because it does not obstruct the view. Next in popularity are the many variations of the triangular design. This design must be kept in proportion to the dish in which it is made, and it must be made so that it does not obstruct the view. A spiral design, arranged in a round dish, is also lovely for the dinner table. The lines of the design can be made with any flowers or branches that are naturally or easily manipulated into curves so that they form a pinwheel design. (Fig. 50.) A fan-shaped arrangement, elongated and kept low, is another useful dinner-table design.

When flowers are used for a stand-up serving, a tall arrangement is more easily seen and therefore more effective—footed compotes, for instance, placed at one end of the table instead of in the middle.

A pair of arrangements may be employed when the dinner table has been extended. A crescent or triangular design may be handled in the same manner that you would arrange a single floral design. A pair of shells placed back to back are lovely arranged with flowers or fruits for an informal setting.

When the floral designer applies his art to the arrangement of fruits and vegetables, the results are surprising. Fruits, with their vast variety of color, form, and texture, combined with vegetables, foliages, and sometimes flowers, are a constant inspiration for table settings. Fruits may be handled as flowers are. A crescent design of fruits and foliage may be placed in a horizontal manner on a round dish, tray, piece of glass or wood. A wooden burl in a free form serves as a lovely base for fruits. (Fig. 51.)

A berried branch combined with fruits will add height to the design. Fruits can be combined harmoniously with flowers, provided there is no sharp division between them. Flowers and foliage can be

Figure 51 A *few green fruits arranged on a wooden burl—like the lime-green grapes and andromeda foliage shown here—serve as a simple fruit arrangement.*

blended gracefully by bringing them together with transitional material. (Plate 17.) The S-curve, also known as the Hogarth curve of beauty, can be very simply executed with fruits. One of my favorite dinner-table arrangements consists of two large bunches of Tokay grapes in an S pattern on a piece of frosted glass that has been tinted on the under side with rose madder oil paint and elevated on a teakwood stand. Echeveria rosettes, slightly tinged at the edges with the rosy hue of the grapes, are used in the center as a focal point, and of course the table linen is related in color to the fruit. (Plate 18.) This same arrangement may be made with fruit of a dark blue or pale green color. With dark blue grapes, a focal point of pink chrysanthemums in place of the echeveria is most effective. Dark green ivy leaves may be artistically interwoven with the fruit. When this same design is made using green grapes, the addition of yellow roses and yellow croton foliage will result in a harmonious and charming design.

Designing with plant material to decorate the home is not just a hobby or a luxurious pastime. It places the homemaker in the role of creative artist and surrounds home and family with a special aura of living beauty.

7

Flowers Arranged for Show

Winning in a flower-show competition requires more than a knowledge of design, color, and the ability to make the flowers stand in
place. A composition made for show must stand out from other
well-designed arrangements because of a quality called "distinction."
This descriptive adjective means different things to different people
and, like a chameleon, the distinguishing quality changes according
to the background. A floral design in competition often has distinction in a greater or lesser degree in relation to competing arrangements.

Bizarre effects do not give a floral design distinction, nor do
exotic and rare flowers always "turn the trick." What, then, is the
recipe for creating designs of distinction with plants and flowers?
Distinction may be achieved by the clever interpretation of the
flower-show schedule—by an unusual flower container, an interesting
or subtle combination of colors, harmonious foliage that is perfectly
related to flowers and receptacle. Sometimes an accessory to the composition may be the instrument through which the design gains
distinction. My personal formula for designing flower-show winners
is to transform ordinary foliages and flowers into designs of extraor-

dinary line and color harmony. I have found that "simplicity" and "distinction" are often synonomous. (Fig. 52.)

One of the fastest ways to acquire experience in arranging flowers for show is to join a garden club and enter all the competitions. In this way you will learn through practice and can benefit from unbiased criticism. Competitive flower showing is a real sport that unfortunately not everyone is temperamentally able to enjoy. Competition of this kind takes imagination, orderly organization of ideas, perseverance, physical energy, and the ability to take criticism graciously. It is surprising how many people have all the qualifications except the last, as anyone who has had flower-show experience knows. There should be a rule written into every flower-show schedule: "The judge's decision is final—alibis and post-mortems not allowed after the show!"

There is a difference in the kinds of flower arrangements made for home decoration and those made for the flower show. Flower designs made for exhibition have limitations and qualifications dictated by the flower-show schedule, which is a program that lists the numbers and names of the entry classes. The artistic part of the schedule is generally divided into numbered classes. For example, "Class 1 may have the title 'Welcome Home,' an arrangement of fresh cut plant material for the entrance hall in the home." The schedule also contains special information for exhibitors about dimensions of the space allowed for each exhibit, background color, and special definitions and rules to make certain the exhibitor understands. For example, "Fresh cut plant material includes berried branches and fruits," or "Dried plant material is allowed in Class X."

It may seem superfluous to mention the importance of reading this program very carefully before planning an exhibit for competitive show, but I have seen some wonderful arrangements lose out because the schedule was not properly read by the exhibitor. On the judges' score sheet often twenty or twenty-five points are allowed for proportion and balance of the design. If the size of the space specified for your exhibit is stated clearly in the schedule and you have read it, you have an opportunity to win these points. Before the show a piece of paper cut the size of the space allowed for your exhibit may be fastened against a wall with Scotch tape and your flower arrangement placed in front of it to be sure your design is in good proportion and scale. It helps to rehearse your design at home before the competitive showing.

Figure 52 *To gain distinction, the design should be kept simple. White ornithogalum lilies, white lupin, gray-green hen and chicken in a clear crystal dish illustrate simplicity and distinction.*

One of the functions of garden clubs is to teach conservation of native plants. Flowers and plants "on conservation" should be listed clearly in the schedule. The exhibitors and committee may have an understanding, however, that if plant material is grown by the exhibitor it may be used for artistic arrangements for show, provided it is labeled to this effect.

A well-written flower-show schedule helps ensure a good show. If a show has a theme, the staging committee may interpret the theme in a manner that will be attractive for the exhibitor as well as the spectator. The following are a few examples of flower-show schedules that have proved attractive and stimulating to the imagination of both the staging committee and exhibitors: "The Circus Comes to Town," "Arts and Flowers," "Fiesta," "Elections of 19–," "———".

Some garden clubs have a flower show each month, and one that I know of had the theme printed in advance in the club's yearbook—"Around the World in 280 Days." Each month the show's schedule included interesting and imaginative classes about various countries of the world.

If you wish to be a consistent winner at the flower show, you must be well organized and prepared. To make a prize-winning exhibit, plans are often made many weeks in advance of the show in order to co-ordinate all the necessary elements. For a design of distinctive beauty, the exhibitor often makes his own flower container, and it is not unusual to find flower-arrangement enthusiasts interested in ceramics and metalcraft. They become adept at making exactly the kind of receptacle or accessory needed for their floral compositions. I remember attending a noisy class in metalcraft many years ago in order to make a pewter plate for a very special exhibition. (Plate 19.) Another time, a Christmas flower show inspired me to try my hand at designing and modeling a round, white, crackled-glaze pottery jar that I had visualized as a receptacle for an arrangement of white poinsettias. (Fig. 53.) The ballerinas and dish that they dance around were designed and modeled for a non-competitive exhibition in New York City many years ago. (Fig. 54.)

Winning the blue ribbon may be a matter of luck once or twice, but consistent winners usually have special "know-how." They may even painstakingly grow flowers and foliages to obtain just the right flower form, texture, and color to carry out their designs. My garden is filled with interesting flowers and foliages that I planted there because of their usefulness to me in bringing the right touch to a flower arrangement.

The design value of foliage in a flower arrangement cannot be emphasized enough. Nine times out of ten it is the foliage that enhances the beauty of the flowers, creates the line of the pattern, relates the arrangement to the receptacle through color and texture, and helps the designer win a prize in the flower show. (Plate 20.) I use the term "foliage" loosely, because I consider branches of shrubs and trees, grasses, berried or fruited vines in the foliage category. You will be doing yourself an injustice if you do not become acquainted with as many varieties of foliages, shrubs, and trees that can help you make unlimited designs with flowers.

Figure 53   A Christmas flower-show schedule in-
spired me to try my hand at designing and modeling a round white crackle-glaze pottery jar as a
receptacle for an arrangement of white poinsettias.

Figure 54 *The ballerinas and the dish they dance around were designed and modeled for an invitation exhibit at the International Flower Show in New York by Lizbeth Schaeffler, ceramic artist. They have been inspiring to work with ever since.*

My experience has been with foliages that grow in the gardens in the northeastern part of the United States.

Andromeda Japonica
Apple
Artemisia
Azalea
Baptisia foliage
Bleeding Heart (Dicentra)
    (both rock garden and
      regular)

Broccoli
Cabbage (Chinese)
Canna foliage
Cherry
Chestnut
Cotoneaster
Climbing rose foliage
Day-lily foliage

Dill
Dusty Miller (Centaurea)
Euonymus
Ferns
Forsythia
Galax
Geranium
High-bush Blueberry
Iris foliage
Ilex
Ivy
Juniper
Laurel
Leucothoë
Lilac
Maple
Mullein
Myosotis—grandiflora foliage
    (perennial forget-me-not)
Pachysandra
Peach

Pear
Pine (black, white, flat needle)
Plum
Pussy Willow
Kitten's Ear
Quince
Raspberry
Rhododendron
Rhubarb
Rhubarb Chard
Rosa Hugonis
Russian Olive
Saxifrage
Sedums—many varieties
Skunk Cabbage
Taxus
Vibernums
Weigela
Wisteria
Witch Hazel

A thriving business in tropical foliages has been stimulated by the flower arrangers' demand for this plant material.

Anthurium
Cacti and a large variety
    of succulents
Caladium
Camellia
Coconut
Crepe Myrtle
Croton
Date
Dieffenbachia
Dracaena
Eucalyptus
Galax
Leucadendron

Ligustrum
Oleander
Palm (Date, Palmetto, Thatch,
    and other varieties)
Philodendron
Pittosporum
Podocarpus
Sansevieria
Scotch Broom
Sea Grape
Southern Magnolia
Strelitzia and
    Calla foliage
Ti

Some of the most dramatic design effects can be obtained with wild flowers and foliages. If you are fortunate enough to live in an area where there are fields and swamps, there is a wealth of plant material to be discovered for its beauty and design value.

Skunk-cabbage blossoms that poke through the mud in the early spring have been a much-admired part of many spring flower arrangements. The large yellow-green leaves that follow the blossom are very handsome, but they are tender and must be carefully conditioned. In the same swamp may be found marsh lilies, whose blossom is of no consequence but whose foliage grows in most perfect design. Cattails and grasses are also appreciated by flower artists for their design value.

In the fields and by the roadside, spikes of dock that change from green to rose and then to brown; gray-green velvety-textured mullein that grows in large rosette-like clusters; milkweed in blossom and later with its seed pods; the rich, rusty brown cones of sumac—these are only a few of the many hundreds of wild-plant materials that are interesting and beautiful for floral design.

I remember assisting a friend who was giving a very large party one summer. We gathered bunches of Queen Anne's Lace and tall spikes of mullein flowers to supplement the flowers ordered to be arranged by a professional for the occasion. When I attended the party I noted that the professional florist had used all the wild material to good advantage. In fact, the most distinctive arrangement in the house was one made of the large blue and purple hybrid delphinium accented with large clusters of gray mullein foliage.

No cultivated flower in the garden is more beautiful than Queen Anne's Lace. Its delicacy of texture and form is most effectively related to crystal. When each blossom is handled with the same care given a rarer bloom, it takes on an air of elegance.

The deserts of Arizona, the sand dunes of Florida, and the swamplands of Louisiana have a wealth of native plant material that has been given the spotlight by local flower arrangers. (Fig. 55.)

Planning on paper is the only practical way to prepare for competitive flower showing. A memorandum with a description of the vase, flowers, foliages, branches, accessories, color scheme, size of space, and name and number of the classes should include a simple line drawing of your arrangement. (Fig. 56.)

If you do not have a garden from which to cut your plant mate-

Figure 55 *The deserts of Arizona, the sand dunes of Florida, and the swamps of Louisiana have a wealth of plant material that has been given the spotlight by local flower arrangers. African silver leaf (Leucadendron), variegated rubber leaves, and a single chrysanthemum are arranged in a Swedish pewter sphere.*

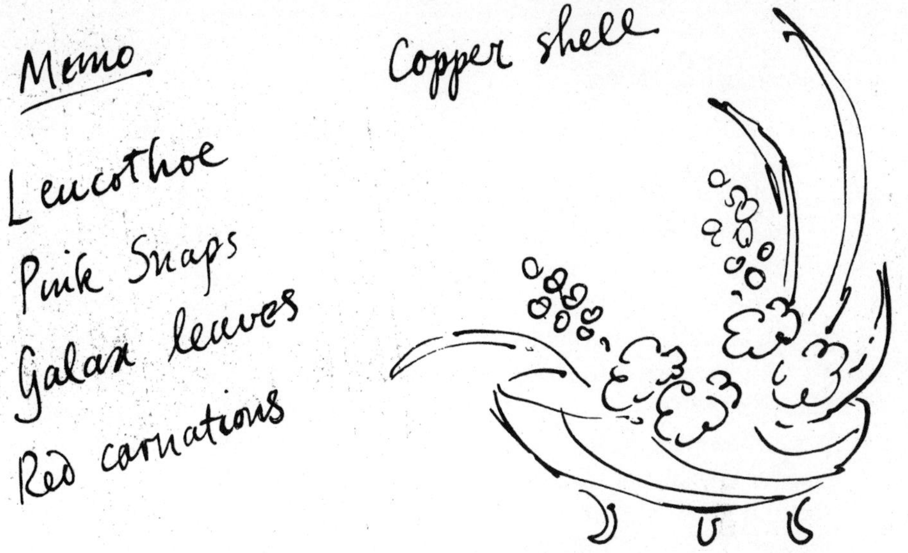

Figure 56 *Flower-show arrangement memo.*

rial, flowers should be ordered at least a week in advance of the show from a florist or nursery.

CONDITIONING

Another extremely important step in preparing for flower show-ing is conditioning the plant material. Even the most experienced exhibitors sometimes make the mistake of using flowers or foliages that have not been conditioned. It is disappointing to lose out just because of wilted plant material. Cut all foliage and flowering ma-terial the day before the show, either in the early morning or late afternoon, when the sun has gone down. Burn or boil stems of varieties that require this special treatment (dahlias, poppies, poin-settias, etc.) Place in deep cool water (do not submerge the blooms) in a cool, dark room. If the stems are woody, like those of lilac or stock, split them at the end for about two inches. If a budded tip wilts, cut the stem with a sharp knife while the stem is still under water and leave it in water for at least five or six hours to allow the wilted part to recuperate. Many flowers and foliage cannot stand the shock of cutting without this special treatment. Rather than take a chance, it is advisable to cut all stems with a sharp shears or knife while the stem is held under water. This allows the water to reach the entire plant without a vacuum caused by the intake of air. (See Fig. 40.) Even flowers that come directly from the florist should be conditioned in this way. Often flowers the florist has just received from market are shipped out to fill orders before he has had a chance to cut the stems.

There are ways of transporting flowers, receptacles, and accessories to the exhibition hall with a minimum of trouble and breakage. If you are permitted to make flower arrangements at home and bring them to the show finished, they may be transported in a corrugated paper box with newspaper stuffed around the container to keep it steady. Wax paper wrapped around the arranged flowers and pinned securely will make the entire package easy to transport and will keep flowers from becoming bruised or broken. A separate small basket for flower shears, knife, wire, pin holders, Scotch tape, floral clay, and other engineering equipment keeps tools conveniently at hand when constructing designs at the show.

Unless you have made your entries in advance, as is customary in the big shows, check the class in the schedule that you wish to enter. When you arrive at the show it will save time if you give your checked schedule, with your name on it, to the entries chairman, who will make out cards to accompany each of your exhibits. It is important to be sure that your entry-card class number corresponds with the number in the schedule and that your arrangements are staged in the right class.

In fairness to everyone concerned, it is best that the exhibitor leave the exhibition hall before the judges arrive. Having judged shows for many years, I know how disconcerting it is to see the owner of an exhibit identifying herself with it by fussing over it after the judges are invited in to start the judging.

The development of good judges for flower-show exhibitions has been one of the aims of the National Council of State Garden Clubs in the United States. Prospective judges have been required to take five courses of lectures and pass a written examination and a practical one in judging a show with each of the five courses in order to receive a certificate stating that they are qualified to judge a flower show. It takes more than five flower-show lecture courses to produce a good judge. In addition to a certificate of qualification, a flower-show judge should have had experience as a successful exhibitor, should have an appreciation of originality, the ability to think independently, and a generosity of spirit.

It is customary to invite three people to judge a flower show. Horticultural experts usually judge specimen blooms and plants, and flower-arrangement specialists judge the artistic section. If the show is very large and there are many classes to be judged, it is advisable to have two or three sets of judges.

Most flower-show judging is carried on with decorum and general agreement. There are times, however, when one of the judges may be so persuasive that the other two members of the team have difficulty making a decision. Although it is the accepted etiquette that the clerks who accompany the judges have nothing to say during the judging, it has always seemed important to me that someone in authority instruct the judges to point-score the arrangement in order to facilitate fair judgment. A good practice is to have the point-scoring for each class or set of classes printed in the flower-show schedule. Exhibitors and judges alike may then use the same set of standards. For example, "Outdoor Table Setting." (Fig. 57.)

POINTS FOR JUDGING:

1. Interpretation of the schedule	20
2. Distinction and originality	20
3. Over-all design (balance, proportion, scale)	15
4. Artistic perfection of centerpiece	20
5. Relationship of all parts in texture and color	15
6. Condition of plant material	10
	100

DESIGNING THE SHOW

Designing the layout for a flower show is like setting the stage for a play. The set must have balance, proportion, scale, color harmony, and a focal point where the theme of the show is made apparent. The theme should be written to stimulate the imagination and interest of the artist as well as the audience. A show schedule is like the playwright's script. Classes may be compared to acts in which the artists perform. Each class is written to inspire dramatization of designs made with plants and flowers.

A flower-show setting may have an over-all form—it may be circular, oval, rectangular, or crescent-shaped. (Fig. 58.) The pattern within the form is usually designed with the properties necessary for staging the show. For example, the flower show mentioned above

Figure 57   *An informal outdoor luncheon table that won a blue ribbon and tricolor at the International Flower Show was composed of a chartreuse-green cloth, Spode Reynolds plates, amethyst glass goblets, and a fruit arrangement that included passionflower vine and buds, pale green-yellow ranunculus, dark blue grapes, nectarines, limes, and green pears.*

with the circus theme was staged in an oval form with a circular central motif.

Whether for prize or for fun, flower showing finds the flower arranger at the top of his form. (Fig. 59.) Sometimes it is puzzling why so many people are willing to put forth so much effort to display such a fragile art. It is only the initiated, those who have experienced the opening-night excitement that comes with the display of an artistic expression even when the artist's medium is flowers, who can give you the answer!

Plate 18   *Two bunches of Tokay grapes arranged on a piece of frosted glass that has been tinted on the under side and a few rosettes of echeveria foliage help to create a Hogarth curve of beauty suitable to adorn the most elegant dinner table.*

Plate 19 *The pewter plate is well related in color and texture to the arrangement of spiral eucalyptus, heather, and echeveria foliage in the above design made for a special flower-show school exhibition.*

Plate 20 *Foliage enhances the beauty of a floral design and often creates the line of a pattern. Sometimes it relates the arrangement to the receptacle through color and texture. Foliage often helps the designer win a prize in a flower show.*

Plate 21 *My impression of the Ohara School. The Ohara School was the first to break away from the traditional ikebana in urn-shaped containers. Strelitzia blossoms and salome philodendron arranged in blue Chinese pottery illustrate my impression of the Moribana style.*

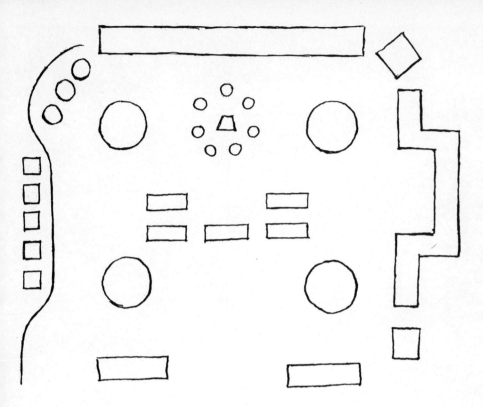

Figure 58   *Flower-show plan.*

WILD FLOWERS, TREES, AND SHRUBS TO BE PRO-HIBITED IN PUBLIC FLOWER SHOWS IN THE NINTH DISTRICT, FEDERATED GARDEN CLUBS OF NEW YORK STATE

(Revised June, 1953)

Arethusa—*Arethusa bulbosa*
Azaleas—Pinxter (*nudiflorum*)
   Swamp (*viscosum*)
Baneberry—Red—*Actaea rubra*
   White—*Actaea alba*
Bittersweet—*Celastrus scandens*
Black Alder—*Ilex verticillata*
Butterfly Weed—*Asclepias tuberosa*

Calopogon—*Calopogon pulchellus*
Canada Lily—*Lilium canadense* (Meadow Lily)
Cardinal Flower—*Lobelia cardinalis*
Checkerberry—*Gaultheria procumbens*

Figure 59 *Whether for prize or for fun, flower showing finds the flower arranger at the top of her form. Blue-ribbon table set for the New York State Federation Garden Clubs 9th District Flower Show, County Center, White Plains, N.Y.*

Club Mosses—*Lycopodiaceae*
  Ground Pine—*Lycopodium camplanatum*; Ground Cedar, etc.
Dwarf Cornel—*Cornus canadensis* (Bunch Berry)

Ferns must be protected if they are on this rare list:

Beechferns—*Phegopteris connectilis, hexagonoptera,* etc.
Climbing—*Lygodium palmatum*

Ebony Spleenwort—*Asplenium platyneuron*

Grapeferns—*Botrychium obliquum, multifidum, etc.*

Hartstongue—*Phyllitis scolopendrium*

Maidenhair—*Adiantum pedatum*

Oakfern—*Currania dryopteris*

Polypody—*Polypodium virginianum*

Rattlesnake Fern—*Botrychium virginianum*

Royal—*Osmunda regalis*

Spleenworts—*Asplenium resiliens,* etc.

Holly, Native American

Ilex opaca. (Cultivated species grown in nurseries for the Christmas green trade can be used.)

Ladies' Tresses—*Spiranthes spp.*

Marsh Marigold—*Caltha palustris*

May Apple—*Podophyllum peltatum*

Moccasin Flowers—*Cypridedium acaule, pubescens, parviflorum, reginae*

Mountain Laurel—*Kalmia latifolia*

Partridge Berry—*Mitchella repens*

Pipsissewa—
Green—*Chimaphila umbellata*
Striped or mottled—*Chimaphila maculata*

Pitcher Plant—*Sarracenia purpurea*

Rattlesnake Plantain—*Goodyera spp.*

Shin-Leaf—*Pyrola elliptica*

Walking Fern—*Camptosorus rhizophyllus*

Woodsia—*Woodsia spp.*

But the common ferns may be used by flower arrangers when grown in a private garden:

Bead Fern—*Onoclea sensibilis* (Sensitive Fern)

Brake, common—*Pteridium latiusculum*

Christmas—*polystichum acrostichoides*

Cinnamon—*Osmunda cinnamomea*

Hay-scented—*Dennstaedtia punctilobula*

Interrupted—*Osmunda claytoniana*

Lady—*Athyrium angustum,* etc.

Ostrich—*Pteretis nodulosa*

Flowering Dogwood—*Cornus florida*

Fringed Orchis—*Habenaria spp.*

Fringed Polygala—*Polygala paucifolia*

Gentians
Closed—*Gentiana andrewski*
Fringed—*Gentiana crinita*
Hepatic—*Hepatica americana*

Showy Orchid—*Orchis spectabilis*

Sweet-scented Water Lily—*Nymphaea odorata*

Trailing Arbutus—*Epigaea
repens*
Trillium—*spp.*
Violets—
  Bird's Foot—*Viola pedata*
  Downy Yellow—*Viola pubes-
cens*

Wild Columbine—**Aquilegia**
canadensis
Wild Orange-red Lily—*Lilium
philadelphicum*

With these recommendations: We believe that all the plants on the list be *allowed in the Horticultural competition of club shows* and in terrariums, *or in educational exhibits, with the exception of those plants that are harmed by picking the flowers and leaves:* the moccasin flowers and the orchid family (wild), and the club mosses.

Growers of wild material will be encouraged and plants increased whereas complete prohibition will discourage propagation. This is our solution for the increasing destruction of our native material, which is very much a part of our heritage, through expansion, road and housing developments, and industrial growth—*let us encourage and build public sanctuaries and private home wild gardens all over our district.*

It is suggested that flower arrangers bear in mind that most wild material does not last well indoors, that lily stems should be cut only half their length to leave foliage to ripen the bulb, and that wherever a club decides to allow material on this list in its *private club shows* because of local conditions of plenty *a proper sign be displayed by the arrangements stating that this material on the conservation list has been grown in the exhibitor's own or a private garden.*

References: *Wild Flower Guide*, Wherry, E. T.
  Guide to Eastern Ferns, Wherry, E. T.
  Growing Woodland Plants, Birdsey, Clarence and Eleanor G.

8

Design with Flowers
East and West

There is a great difference between the art of designing with flowers in the West and the art of designing with flowers in Japan. In the West the art is practiced mostly by women and used for interior decoration in the home. In Japan a flower arrangement is placed in the *tokonoma* (alcove) or any other part of the home as a simple expression of beauty and may have no connection with room decoration. Like the beautiful thoughts contained in some old scroll hanging on the wall in a Japanese home, the few branches and flowers placed in a vase have a message of beauty that is as important to the Japanese soul as the sun is to a flower.

It took me many weeks before I finally appreciated the fact that *ikebana* (flower arrangement) in Japan is not just a "domestic art." There were many people in Tokyo who believed that it may have had something to do with the religious philosophy of the people many years ago but was now just "big business." I learned differently. I found that *ikebana* is so much a part of every Japanese person that it has helped mold the Japanese character.

Long before I went to Japan I had always had a reverent attitude toward an arrangement of flowers designed in the Japanese style. My first instruction in flower arranging was given to me by a Japanese lady in the United States in 1937, and my first inspiration came from a few books written in English on the technique of various schools of Japanese flower arranging. There was something so perfect about the simplicity of this Japanese art that whenever I viewed an arrangement made by a Japanese person I had a feeling that this beauty was conceived from love and devotion. Many years ago in the United States I studied the ways of making holders, called *kubaris*, to support the flowers. I learned how the branches were manipulated to curve in a more dramatic flow of line than Nature intended. But I never learned the philosophy underlying the art of Japanese flower arranging until I went to Japan. All through the years I had a hankering to go there, the source from which my love for design with flowers originated.

It was a thrill to walk up to the Golden Pavilion called Kinkaku-ji, in Kyoto and know that it was in this very garden four hundred years ago that Saomi, the famous artist of his day, conceived the idea of making the temple and shrine offerings of flowers, designs of beautiful line and significant meaning. I knew from books I had read that Yoshimasa, the great shogun of the Ashikaga Dynasty, who lived about the time Columbus discovered America (1436–90), was a great patron of the arts, and it was during his reign that the Golden Pavilion was built and that Saomi was commissioned to make his wonderful paintings. Yoshimasa finally abdicated in order to devote his life to the arts and cultures of his country and the development of them. He felt very keenly that the floral offerings made in the temples should be a real expression of beauty and should be given much thought and have significant meaning. Rules were made to guide the people in making these floral offerings, and further refinements were added. Teachers, whom the Japanese call *senseis*, sprang up to serve the community temples.

Credit for applying the elements Heaven, Man, and Earth to the lines of a flower arrangement is attributed to Saomi, the painter. The first temple arrangements were massive affairs, called *rikkwa*, in large urns. There is a revival of interest in *rikkwa* in Japan today. When I visited an exhibition in Tokyo it was my good fortune to see an elderly man dismantle a *rikkwa* arrangement he had constructed for display. In the center of most *rikkwa* arrangements is a large, almost tree-like piece of evergreen material, which represents the distant scenery, and a flowering shrub, which represents the close view. (Fig. 60.) These first arrangements were known as *shin-no-*

Figure 60 *The first Japanese temple arrangements were massive affairs in large urns called* rikkwa.

Figure 61 *Bamboo holder for* rikkwa *arrangement.*

Figure 63 *Two styles of Japanese* kubaris.

Figure 64 *Right and left sided aspidistra leaves.*

Figure 67 Kubari *for Enshu School.*

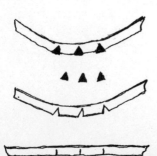

Figure 69 *Slits are made and wooden wedges inserted to make a stiff branch curve.*

hana. Today the first and most important branch or flower in a Japanese classical or modern flower arrangement is called the *shin* branch. The *shin* branch is the equivalent of the Heaven line. The mechanics the elderly designer used to keep these heavy branches together and in an upright position was a first-rate piece of engineering. Large pieces of bamboo, cut and fastened together with wires, were the holders in which the large branches were secured. (Fig. 61.)

Cha-no-yu, the Tea Ceremony, and *Koawase,* the Incense Ceremony, were all a part of Yoshimasa's program to bring real beauty of rhythm and design into the Buddhist ritual. Every prayer was one of thanksgiving for the bounties of Nature and a deep wish to be blessed with further bounties the sun provided. The shrines and temples were not always located near enough for the average farmer to visit often, so in every home it became the custom to build an alcove, or *tokonoma.* In this small shrine hangs a scroll the Japanese call a *kakemono,* and on a slightly elevated floor is placed some object of beauty prized by the owner. A small urn for incense, a wood carving, a beautiful stone, a bit of ceramic art, or even just a lovely teacup may be chosen for this place of honor, and of course the simple but beautiful flower arrangement. Often the scroll bears only calligraphy —beautifully formed characters that translate into poetry or the philosophy by which the family lives. The flower arrangement is made to indicate the respect and love of Nature within the home and is a part of the Tea Ceremony, which is a ritual performed in front of the *tokonoma.*

It is true that Japan is modern in its thinking today. Large factories, office buildings, and modern department stores are very much in the foreground in the large cities. The young couples who can afford to build homes are building modern structures. However, in every contemporary Western-style home I saw in Tokyo there was always one room in the old tradition—the "*tatami* room." The floor matting, known as *tatami,* gives the room its name. In this room is a *tokonoma,* with its flower arrangement and *kakemono,* or scroll. One young couple told me they found they spent most of their time in their *tatami* room "because it is so comfortable, relaxing, and beautiful." I know this is true—I lived in a *tatami* room when I was in Japan.

To gain a better knowledge of Japanese flower arrangement in modern Japan I studied in four of the leading schools in Tokyo. The senior *senseis* from the Ohara and Sogetsu schools spoke English very well, and before their big schools started in the fall they were able to give me private instruction in my *tatami* room. I learned from them the slight differences in these two modern schools—differences mainly in the names given the main branches in the arrangements and in the names of the styles of the first patterns as prescribed by the masters in each school. After learning the prescribed patterns, the flower arranger can use his own imagination and make designs in all kinds of patterns suggested by the flower container and the material. Arrangements made in abstract designs with all kinds of live plant material are very popular. Often wire and strips of metal were used instead of branches, with few or no flowers to complete the design. (Fig. 62.)

The Sogetsu school, whose master, Mr. Sofu Teshigahara, is a modern artist with great imagination, built a beautiful modern structure to house his school. In addition to classrooms, it has a small theater and a terrace decorated with interesting stone and metal sculpture. I attended a meeting and large reception held in the Sogetsu Art Center one evening, and the lovely ladies in their traditional Japanese kimonos were in strong contrast to the extreme modern surroundings. This is characteristic of Japan today—a blending of old and new. Even in the modern Sogetsu school, Mr. Sofu has a special *tatami* room built for the express purpose of teaching the ancient Tea Ceremony.

The other important modern school in Tokyo, the Ohara school, has a large, fine structure with classrooms and many extra meeting rooms. The Ohara school was the first to break away from the traditional Ikenobo school, which advocated making arrangements in urnshaped containers rather than in the low *moribana* dish style. (Plate 21.) Mr. Ohara's grandfather was the rebel who created this new school. Today, of course, the *moribana* style of arrangement in a low, flat receptacle is generally accepted in all of the schools of Japanese flower arrangement.

I witnessed the judging of over a hundred exhibits in the Ohara school, all made in the same-shaped vase with the same plant material, arranged in the *nageire* style. I should hate to have had the job of judging these exhibits. They all looked so good, and there was such a variety of result, in spite of the uniformity of the vases and the plant material.

I was told that the masters of the modern schools consider flower arrangements made in the classical style suitable only for the *toko-*

Figure 62 *My impression of Sogetsu style. Arrangement made in bisque pottery using imported dried Japanese mulberry vines and chrysanthemums.*

noma. They believe that their work fills a current need for modern design expressed with flowers. I had the feeling that although there is a tremendous interest and many followers of the Sogetsu and Ohara schools, the Ikenobo and Enshu schools will always remain to represent *ikebana* in the old Japanese tradition. Even in these schools, where the kinds of branches and how they are arranged are dictated by tradition, my teachers (through an interpreter) told me they enjoyed working in the modern style and proudly showed me pictures of their work in the traditional schools of Ikenobo and Enshu done with a modern twist.

The Ikenobo school, whose young headmaster is a direct descendant of the school's originator, resides in Kyoto. My *sensei* in this school in Tokyo was a little Japanese lady who was preceded each morning by the florist. The florist's bundle always contained her order for the branches and flowers suitable for the day's lesson. On top of the bundle there was usually a nice straight branch, made of just the right kind of wood and shorn of all foliage. This is the wood from which the *kubari* is traditionally cut for the Ikenobo school. (Fig. 63.) Aspidistra leaves are often used for traditional *ikebana,* and during my course of instructions the florist had the leaves already bundled so that the right- or left-hand leaves could be selected easily. It seems that some aspidistra leaves grow with the broader side on the left and some with the broader side on the right of the center vein. (Fig. 64.) The words for "right" and "left" became a part of my Japanese vocabulary very soon. I found that *migi,* meaning right, and *hidari,* meaning left, came in very handy, not only in describing *migi-bana,* a right-handed flower arrangement, and *hidari-bana,* a left-handed arrangement, but in directing the taxi drivers in Tokyo, who seldom spoke English. Being able to say these words made it easier for me to direct them to where I wanted to go.

Beautiful and simple flower containers made of bamboo were the earliest vases for flowers in the Japanese classical schools. In the Ikenobo, one of the oldest traditional schools, the bamboo flower container is still used with great artistry and variety today. Bamboo in simple, straight cylinders, some cut with small windows or second sections, and even some made in the shape of a boat, are traditional with the Ikenobo school. (Fig. 65.) Bronze containers designed for the Ikenobo school are usually a little heavier and of simpler lines than the bronze containers used in the Enshu school. (Fig. 66.)

Figure 65   *Impression of Ikenobo style. A bamboo cylinder cut with small window is called a niju. The flowers are arranged in one of the oldest traditional patterns.*

Figure 66 *My impression of Ikenobo style. The classical style is still popular for arrangements made in the tokonoma. Flat-needle pine and calla lilies are arranged in the traditional bronze container characteristic of the Ikenobo school.*

The *moribana* style is a relatively new innovation but makes use of the same holder that is suitable for an Ikenobo arrangement. This *kubari* is made with a forked stick that fits into a special heavy metal ring which can be placed in a flat dish.

Since the Japanese woman who had given me my first lessons in Japanese flower arrangement in the United States had studied in the Enshu school as a little girl, I was particularly anxious to learn more of the technique of arranging flowers in this classical school. I was surprised to learn that there are practically no teachers in the Enshu school in Tokyo today, but after many inquiries I finally located Mr. Mori, a florist and *sensei* of the Enshu school in Yokohama. Never have I seen such deft, wonderful hands. The speed with which he worked as he went about sawing the wood to make the special type of holder that is characteristic of the Enshu school was absolutely miraculous. He cut two pieces of teak-wood molding and a thin piece of plywood, which he placed between, at just the right length to fit securely into the top of a tall vase or the metal rim that is usually a part of the Japanese bronze containers. He bound wire around the end of the holder to hold the wood tightly together. When completed, the holder acted as a slot into which the sharply cut wedge-shaped ends of the branches were placed. (Fig. 67.) "About a hand-spread" was the way he told me to measure the amount of stem to be cleaned of foliage. This branch must have a natural straight growth (or the possibility of being manipulated so that it looks like a natural straight growth). "Two hand-spreads" measured the point at which the arranger starts to bend the *shin*, or Heaven, branch to form the first curve.

The Enshu school is known for the special technique and artistry with which the branches are manipulated. (Fig. 68.) When the wood is very heavy and brittle, small slits are made in the branch at the points where the arranger wants the wood to bend. From a separate piece of wood of the same size and kind, small notches or wedges are cut. By carefully bending the slits open and inserting the wooden wedges, a natural-looking curve may be made in what might have been a straight, stiff branch. (Fig. 69.) When more supple branches are used, like the willow, beautiful curves can be manipulated by carefully twisting and pulling as the branch is bent. This takes great care, time, and patience, but the results can be very gratifying.

Because of the practice necessary to become proficient in the technique required in the Enshu school, it takes longer to receive a

Figure 68 *My impression of Enshu style. The Enshu School is known for the special technique and artistry with which branches are manipulated. An arrangement of pussy willows and spider chrysanthemums arranged in a bronze* usabata *is characteristic.*

certificate in this school. It is not uncommon for the average Japanese student to take two to three years just to receive a beginner's certificate. Perhaps this is one of the reasons the Enshu school has lost some of its following.

Learning in the Enshu school in Japan was a very pleasant experience for me, especially because I had had previous training and interest in it. The Enshu style of Japanese flower arrangement requires such artistry, it is no wonder that it is a challenge to our Western flower arrangers who try to imitate this classical style. Cyprus, willow, Scotch broom, pine, juniper, and taxus, as well as aspidistra leaves, are suitable plant material for classical *ikebana*.

Learning the technique of arranging branches and flowers in four schools of Japanese flower arranging was considered somewhat of a stunt and one that no Japanese in his right mind would tackle. I was forgiven for attempting this feat, first because I was a "foreign lady," and second because I was an *ikebana sensei* (flower-arrangement teacher) in the United States. This gave me a sort of head start on the foreigner who learns *ikebana* for the first time in Japan. My flower arrangements at home had always been original creations, influenced only by the rules and regulations that govern good design. It was quite a departure from what I had been doing for so many years to be told suddenly that if you placed No. 1 branch at a certain angle and No. 2 branch at another angle and No. 3 branch looking in still another direction, the result would be a named style of flower arrangement.

I felt the deepest humility and a sincere wish to learn at firsthand as much as I could about the techniques of Japanese flower art; but, more than that, I wanted to learn the philosophy underlying the art. I asked everyone, "What does *ikebana* mean to you?" I received a variety of answers. Each of my teachers gave me pretty much the same answer: "Maybe at one time *ikebana* was a part of the philosophy, but today . . ." They looked wistful, as if they questioned it. After a while I felt almost as if I were seeking an ancient treasure that everyone had forgotten. Then suddenly, in a most unexpected place, I found my first clue. I met a beautiful young woman who worked in a night club. When I asked her, "Does flower arrangement mean something special to you? Does it have anything to do with your philosophy?" "You know," she answered after a moment, "I never thought of it that way. All I know is that when I am tired and discouraged after working hard I stop at a little

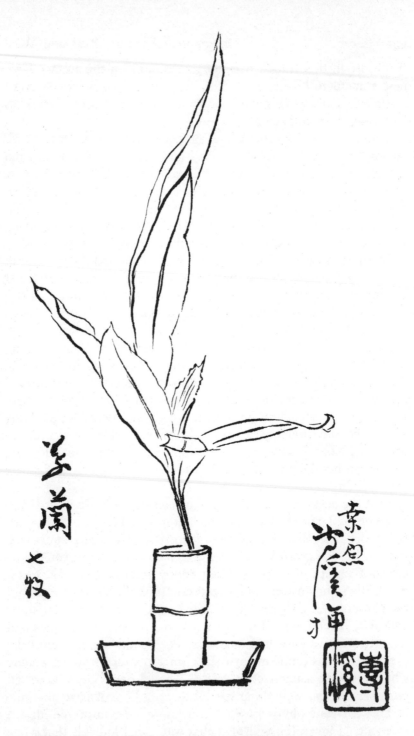

Figure 70 *Mr. Senkei Kuwabara, headmaster of the Kuwabara Senkei Ryu in Kyoto, demonstrated his style with aspidistra leaves in a bamboo cylinder and made a sketch which he signed as a gift to me.*

florist's shop on my way home and buy a few flowers. I go to my room to arrange them. While I am fixing them my problems seem to drop away from me; when I am finished I feel good inside."

I was told by a very intelligent gentleman who worked for the Japanese government that I would probably get my answers in Kyoto, the ancient capital of Japan and still the cultural seat of the nation. I went to Kyoto, and it was while I was there that I felt sure I understood better what *ikebana* means to the Japanese people.

I was quietly seated, taking in the unusual beauty of the rock-and-sand garden of the ancient Ryoan-ji Temple, when I looked about me and realized the Japanese people who had come to view this famous garden of rocks were kneeling on the steps in silence. They seemed to be contemplating the beauty of the garden and silently meditating while they gazed at its artistic perfection.

I had a special invitation to see the Tea Ceremony performed by the masters at the Tea Ceremony School when I was in Kyoto. I had had a little instruction in the performance of this rite, which made it more meaningful to me. Each studied movement has beauty, grace, and purpose. I learned that the Tea Ceremony is another of the rites the Japanese people perform in silent appreciation of beauty.

One evening while I was in Kyoto it was my privilege to visit in the home of the master of a beautiful classical school of *ikebana*, Kuwabara Senkei Ryu (Fig. 70.) Through an interpreter we discussed the philosophy underlying *ikebana*. Mr. Senkei Kuwabara assured me that my observations and deductions were correct. He seemed grateful and surprised at my interest.

We Westerners speak of our "spiritual needs" as if they were unique. An important part of our church service is the time allowed for meditation and prayer. Philosophy that allows for contemplation of beauty and meditation fills the spiritual needs of a people. The Japanese people meditate and contemplate the beauty of Nature and feel closer to it when they are arranging flowers.

Ikebana in Japan is not an art that belongs to just a privileged few. People in all walks of life, all ages, and both sexes are familiar with it. If they have not had the advantage of special schooling in the art, they are sufficiently interested to have made a private study of their own. As children they often learn from their parents.

In the United States flower arranging is a popular art, but it can hardly be called one that is practiced by all the people. In Japan everyone is aware of flowers and how they are placed in a vase. I found flowers "arranged" on information desks in department stores, in tiny restaurants, and even in lavatories on trains—not just flowers stuck in a vase, but flowers thoughtfully arranged.

The young boy and girl who worked in the housekeeping department of the hotel in which I lived spoke Japanese together while they worked at cleaning my room. I could not understand them until they said "Ohara," "Sogetsu," "Ikenobo," and then I knew they were discussing the different schools of flower arrangement. They tried to identify the completed flower arrangements that stood around my room after my lessons were finished for the day. They were amused with the "foreign lady" who was studying in four schools of *ikebana,* all at once.

I was told that in Japan some of the large factories do not give a "coffee break" to their employees, but they do have classes in *ikebana* that the workers can take advantage of. The need for quiet contemplation of beauty and a chance to meditate is more important to the Japanese worker than a cup of tea or coffee. I discussed *ikebana* with the director of one of the largest department stores in Tokyo and also with a professor of philosophy in the university there. A director of one of the large banks, as well as the Foreign Minister, discussed the Japanese art of arranging flowers with a warm, live interest and complete understanding. This is the one Japanese culture that really belongs to all. It would be difficult for the personality of a people not to be affected by this spark of beauty that warms the hearts of all of them.

GLOSSARY

Chan-no-yu: *Tea Ceremony*
Hidari: *left*
Ikebana: *flower arrangement*
Kakemono: *hanging scroll*
Kinka-ku-ji: *name of Golden Pavilion in Kyoto*
Kubari: *flower holder*
Migi: *right*
Moribana: *low dish style of flower arrangement*
Nageire: *falling out style of flower arrangement*
Shin-no-hana: *first flower arrangements*
Rikkwa: *first temple arrangements*
Ryoan-ji: *temple famous for rock and sand garden*
Saomi: *famous Japanese artist 15th century*
Senseis: *teachers*
Tatami: *straw floor matting*
Tokonoma: *alcove in the home*
Yoshimasa: *Shogun of Ashikaga Dynasty (1436–90)*

Flower Color Groups

RED

Tulip
Geranium
Amaryllis
Monarda (Bee Balm)
Sweet William
Carnation
Cockscomb
Morning-Glory
Petunia
Portulaca
Nasturtium
Phlox
Verbena
Salpiglossis
Rose
Azalea
Magnolia
Banana blossom

Skunk-Cabbage blossom
Sweet Pea
Stock
Snapdragon
Chrysanthemums
Anthurium
Torch Ginger
Gladiolus
Anemone
Zinnia
Dahlia
Salvia
Cactus blossom
Poinsettia
Cosmos
Begonia blossom
Primula (Primrose)
Geum

YELLOW

Spring

Tulip dasystemon
Crocus
Daffodil
Tulips of all varieties
Tulip persica
Alyssum (Pot of Gold)
Daisy-type Doronicum caucasi-
   cum

Forsythia (shrub)
Viola and Pansy
Columbine
Iris (Dutch and German
   Bearded)
Trollius
Mahonia (shrub)

Potentilla (June–October)
(shrub)
Rosa Hugonis (shrub)
Hemerocallis (Day-Lily)
Peony (cream)
Peony (tree variety)
Azalea (shrub)
Laburnum Vossii, Golden-
Chain (tree)
Primrose

Hypericum
Ranunculus
Sedum spectabile
Rose
Lupin
Anemone
Kerria (single and double)
(shrub)
Hemerocallis (Day-Lily)
Anthemis (Anthemis Daisy)

Summer

Marigold
Zinnia
Rudbeckia
Eremurus (Foxtail Lily)
Coreopsis (Daisy)
Heliopsis
Snapdragon
Tritoma
Gladiolus
Tuberous Begonia
Trumpet Vine
Primrose (evening, citrous yel-
low)
Iris (Dutch, Japanese, Siberian,
Louisiana)
Geum
Thermopsis
Poppy (Iceland and Cali-
fornia)
Foxglove

Chrysanthemum
Dianthus (Carnation)
Cockscomb
Enkianthus (shrub)
Larkspur
Wallflower
Scabiosa
Stock
Strawflower
Rose
Phlox
Cosmos
Gerbera
Sweet Pea
Chrysanthemum (Cushion,
early Azalea variety)
Calendula
Nasturtium

Fall

Dahlia
Chrysanthemum
Sunflower
Zinnia

Marigold
Cockscomb
Hemerocallis
Statice

Cosmos
Gaillardia

Salpiglossis
Coreopsis

PINK

Verbena
Peony
Rose
Tulip
Scilla
Hyacinth
Lily speciosum
Iris
Poppy
Phlox
Penstemon
Physostegia
Spiraea
Lythrum
Carnation (Dianthus hybrids)
Aster
Dahlia
Celosia—Cockscomb
Cosmos
Four-o'Clock
Cleome
Begonia
Petunia
Snapdragon
Stock
Larkspur
Portulaca
Salvia farinacea
Scabiosa
Azalea
Strawflower
Lupin (Russell)
Chrysanthemum
Anemone
Sweet William

Ajuga
Gypsophila Rosy Veil
Bletilla Hyacinthina (Orchid
    hardy)
Clematis
Cypripedium spectabile
Dicentra spectabilis
Dianthus
Primula japonica
Geranium grandiflorum
Epimedium
Hibiscus
Erianthus Ravennae
Phlox camla
Hemerocallis
Hollyhocks (new double pom-
    padour)
Sedum Sieboldii
Gerbera
Penstemon
Heuchera
Geranium subcaulescens
Lychnis Viscaria flore-pleno
Monarda
Zinnia
Physostegia, Vivid
Platycodon
Hardy Tritoma
Verbascum
Polygonum (Geranium)
Viola (pink and mauve)
Hardy Amaryllis
Amarcrinum
Dahlia
Ranunculus

Canna
Gladiolus
Tuberous Rooted Begonia
Fuchsia
Tamarix
Weigela
Robinia
Weeping Crab
Malus Ioensis (Crab)

Magnolia
Lilac
Flowering Cherry
Hydrangea
Daphne Sumerset
Buddleia
Rhododendron
Almond, Flowering

ORANGE

Tulip
Narcissus
Clivia
Azalea
Calendula
Pansy
Viola
Tritoma
Zinnia
Marigold
Crocus
Geranium
Rose
Anthurium
Amaryllis

Ranunculus
Poppy
Portulaca
Water lily
Lily
Dahlia
Cockscomb
Echeveria blossom
Begonia blossom
Primula
Iris
Nasturtium
English Wallflower
Geum
Snapdragon

BLUE AND VIOLET

Spring

Phlox divaricata
Crocus
Chionodoxa
Scilla
Grape Hyacinth
Mertensia (Virginia Bluebell)
Myosotis (annual and perennial)

Iris
Vine Clematis
Tulip
Ajuga
Columbine
Siberian Iris
Veronica
Violet

Viola
Pansy
Hosta Lily

Baptisia
Wisteria

BLUE

Summer

Delphinium
Columbine
Iris (Japanese)
Campanula
Digitalis (Foxglove)
Platycodon
Larkspur
Aster (annual and perennial)
Veronica
Ajuga
Tradescantia (Widow's-tear)
Scabiosa
Centaurea
Verbena

Ageratum
Lupin
Morning-Glory (heavenly
    blue)
Globe-Flower
Vinca
Lobelia
Petunia
Sweet Pea
Heliotrope
Salpiglossis
Flax
Alyssum

BLUE

Fall

Plumbago
Chrysanthemum
Aconitum
Agapanthus (blue lily-of-the-
    Nile)
Anchusa (Forget-Me-Not)
Torenia

Delphinium
Campanula
Scilla
Iris
Grape Hyacinth
Mertensia

GREEN

Bells of Ireland
Daffodil (new)
Chrysanthemum
Tulip
Christmas Rose

Hydrangea (buds)
Green fruits and berries
Sedum blossoms
Lily buds

Bibliography

Design Fundamentals, Carol J. Felsted; Pitman Publishing Corp., 1958

Art of Color and Design, Maitland Graves; McGraw-Hill Book Co., Inc., 1951

Thoughts on Design, Paul Rand; Wittenborn, Schultz, Inc., 1951

Design Fundamentals, Robert Scott; McGraw-Hill Book Co., Inc., 1951

Language of Design, Charles Watkins; Macmillan Co., 1937

A Color Notation, A. Munsell; Royal B. Farnum, 1946

Science of Color, Optical Society of America and Committee on Colorimetry, 1952

Color Dimensions, Faber Birren; Crimson Press, 1934

Color Harmony, Sterling B. McDonald; Wilcox & Follett Co., 1949

Handbook for Flower Shows, National Council of State Garden Clubs, Inc., 1957

Japanese Flower Arrangement, Mary Averill; Dodd, Mead & Co., 1933

The Art of Japanese Flower Arrangement, Alfred Koehn; J. L. Thompson & Co., Ltd., Japan, and Kegan Paul, Trench, Trubner & Co., London, 1933

Index